Deadly
INVADERS

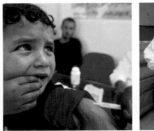

A **New York Times** BOOK

Deadly
INVADERS

Virus Outbreaks Around the World,
from Marburg Fever to Avian Flu

Denise Grady

KINGFISHER

KINGFISHER

Kingfisher Publications
A Houghton Mifflin Company imprint
222 Berkeley Street
Boston, Massachusetts 02116
www.houghtonmifflinbooks.com

First published in 2006
2 4 6 8 10 9 7 5 3
Printed in China
2TR/0407/PROSP/PICA(PICA)/130MA/C

On the cover: Marburg viruses magnified more than 100,000 times.
The type for this book was set in Rotis Semi Sans.
Book design by Anthony Cutting
Cover design by Mike Buckley
Photo research by Maggie Berkvist

Library of Congress Cataloging-in-Publication Data
Grady, Denise.
Deadly invaders: virus outbreaks around the world, from Marburg fever to
avian flu
p. cm.
Includes bibliographical references and index.
ISBN: 978-0-7534-5995-9
1. Virus diseases—Juvenile literature. 2. Emerging infectious
diseases—Juvenile literature. 3. Marburg virus—Juvenile literature.
4. Avian influenza—Juvenile literature. I. Title.
RA644.V55G73 2006
614.5'8—dc22

6/07 B+T $8.85

For Robert, Brian, and Eric.

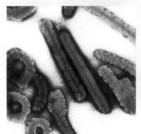
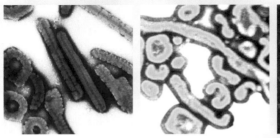
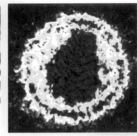
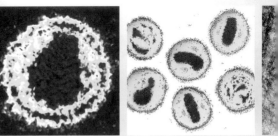

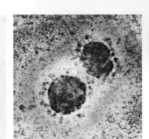
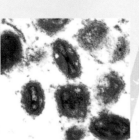

Contents

An Emerging Threat

An illness sweeps the globe. In a matter of months, nearly 2 million people die and another 8.5 million are hospitalized, just in the United States. Makeshift hospitals must be set up in schools and armories because the real ones have run out of space. There are not enough respirators to save all the patients who can't breathe. Riots break out at clinics; vaccine trucks are hijacked. There are power failures and shortages of food and gasoline because utility workers and truck drivers are too sick, or too afraid, to go to work. Morgues and funeral homes are overwhelmed.

That story may sound like a movie plot, but it was actually part of a report issued by government health officials late in 2005, describing what could happen in the United States if there is a flu pandemic—an epidemic that spreads all over the world.

It is humbling and frightening to realize that a seemingly ordinary disease could cause such chaos in a modern, technologically sophisticated country like the United States. But the threat posed by influenza and other infectious diseases is real. The dangers go far beyond illness itself, because epidemics can cause widespread panic and disorder. They can also result in tremendous financial losses as people stay home from work and school and quit doing many other routine things that help keep a nation's economy afloat, such as traveling, shopping, and going to movies and restaurants. The possibility of a flu pandemic has become a major concern for scientists and governments around the world.

The level of alarm about possible outbreaks was not always so high. During the 1960s and part of the 1970s, the United States and other industrialized countries lived in a sort of contented bubble. They believed that infectious diseases would soon be defeated—wiped out or at least brought under control—by vaccines that prevented illness and antibiotics that cured diseases by killing bacteria.

For a while, the idea seemed reasonable enough. Antibiotics to fight illnesses like pneumonia and infection in cuts and wounds came into use during the 1940s. So did flu vaccine. And through the following decades, vaccines were developed to prevent many other viral diseases.

Before the development of these medicines, families had lived in fear that children would be crippled or even killed by polio. Parents had also dreaded a host of unavoidable childhood diseases that could be quite debilitating, including mumps, measles, German measles, and chickenpox.

But by the 1960s, all those diseases except for chickenpox could be prevented by vaccines, and a chickenpox vaccine came later.

Vaccination eradicated the smallpox virus in the United States by 1950, and worldwide by 1980. Vaccines were developed to prevent bacterial diseases as well, including tetanus, diphtheria, and whooping cough. Together, antibiotics and vaccines saved so many children's lives that the average lifespan in America increased dramatically during the twentieth century. In 1900 the average age of death for an American was forty-seven—by 1970 it was seventy-one.

Another way to measure the strides made through vaccinations and antibiotics is to look at death rates in the twentieth century. In 1900, for every 100,000 people, 797 died from an infectious disease. By 1980, the number had dropped to 36 per 100,000—less than a twentieth of the rate at the turn of the century. Much of the improvement was due to medicines.

Given the tremendous achievements made by vaccines and antibiotics, it's understandable that by the 1950s and 1960s even many scientists thought infectious diseases had been conquered, or soon would be.

But during the 1970s scientists began to realize that new outbreaks were cropping up. Some were caused by bacteria and viruses that had never been known before. In others, old germs reached new places or made a comeback after developing resistance to the drugs that used to kill them. Some outbreaks occurred because people stopped using vaccines or could not afford to get them. These often deadly illnesses became known as "emerging infectious diseases." The trend has continued, and scientific

In 1955 a boy is inoculated by Dr. Jonas Salk, developer of the first vaccine against polio.

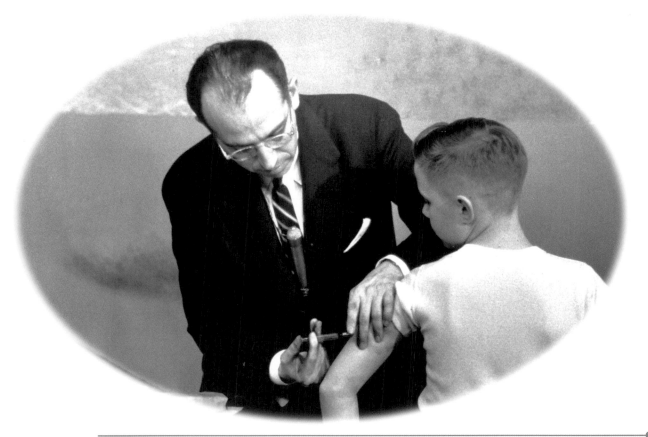

A N E M E R G I N G T H R E A T

advances have made it possible now to hunt down and identify disease agents that might have escaped detection in the past.

Often, though not always, new diseases emerge in developing countries, and when they do, they pose an ethical challenge to richer nations, which many people believe have a moral obligation to help. Whether or not you believe that a humanitarian responsibility exists, there is also a practical, perhaps selfish reason for the rest of the world to try to stop or prevent epidemics in seemingly remote places: nowhere is truly remote anymore. With air travel making it possible for an infected person—or even an animal or insect—to get on a plane and carry germs halfway around the world in a matter of hours, one country's disease can quickly become a deadly invader in another country.

Global trade can spread germs, too. Exotic pets sometimes come bearing equally exotic diseases. Imported food has also caused disease outbreaks in the United States: for example, in 2003, scallions (also called green onions) from Mexico made at least 540 people in Pennsylvania sick with hepatitis A, a viral infection of the liver. Three died.

Airline travel can spread viruses across international borders.

Emerging viruses are among the most worrisome of new germs, because antibiotics do not work against them and there are relatively few antiviral drugs. Not every viral disease can be prevented by a vaccine, and even when one is possible, it can take years to develop. Meanwhile, people fall ill and some die.

In the past few decades, a host of terrifying emerging viral diseases has jolted the world. AIDS, the immune deficiency disease caused by a virus, was first recognized in the United States in 1981. Twenty years later, with more than twenty million dead, the disease has become a worldwide crisis. Bird flu (avian influenza), a severe and deadly type of flu, has been cropping up repeatedly in birds and occasionally in humans since it first appeared in Asia in 1997, sparking fears about the possibility of a deadly pandemic. SARS (severe acute respiratory syndrome), a pneumonia-like viral infection, was first recognized in China in 2003 and was carried by travelers to other parts of Asia and to Canada and the United States before quarantine measures halted its spread.

In the United States, a newly identified member of a family of germs called hantaviruses caused outbreaks of a deadly lung infection in New Mexico, Arizona, and other western states in 1993. West Nile virus, which can cause fever and sometimes a brain infection, encephalitis, was known in the Middle East but had never been found in the United States until 1999, when cases occurred in New York. Since then, it has spread to nearly every state.

Every one of these emerging diseases can cause illness and death, and most pose a real threat to global health. Perhaps the most frightening of the emerging infections are a group of illnesses found in Africa, Asia, and South America called viral hemorrhagic fevers. Two of the worst, found in Africa, are caused by the Ebola and Marburg viruses. Few diseases attack so swiftly or devastatingly. Outbreaks tend to erupt mysteriously, without warning. The viruses, closely related, both cause

WHAT IS A VIRUS?

Viruses are tiny germs, smaller than bacteria or fungi, too small to see with an ordinary microscope. There are thousands of different viruses, and they often cause disease. They can infect people, plants, animals, and even bacteria. Generally, viruses measure just millionths of an inch in diameter. Most bacteria are a hundred to a thousand times bigger.

Viruses have been around for millions of years, but they were first recognized just a little more than a hundred years ago. Scientists had already known about the existence of bacteria, but in the 1870s agricultural researchers in Holland discovered that there were other mysterious disease-causing agents that infected plants and were so small that they could pass through filters that trapped bacteria.

But size is not all that sets viruses apart from other germs. Viruses are unique in that they can't multiply or do much of anything for themselves unless they can get inside the cells of their victims. They can't take in food to produce the energy they would need to grow or repair themselves or move.

In fact, viruses are not even cells. Cells are full of biological machinery that can turn nutrients into energy, make protein, and reproduce. Viruses have none of that. They are stripped down, nothing but a bit of genetic material wrapped in protein, sometimes with a fatty outer coat as well. The genetic material contains the instructions for making more viruses, but not the tools. Because viruses cannot function on their own, scientists have debated about whether they should be counted as alive, or just as lifeless specks of chemicals. There is no definite answer.

In a way, a virus is like a burglar who is trying to break into a chemical plant with only a skeleton key. The burglar has no chemistry set of his own, but if he can get into the factory, he's smart enough to take it over and use it to make deadly poison. Viruses have burglar tools of a sort: keylike attachments that fit into structures on some cells and let the viruses enter. Once they are inside, a frightening transformation takes place. The supposedly lifeless virus becomes an assassin, hijacking the equipment that the cell normally uses to multiply and turning it into a virus factory. Often, the cell dies when armies of viruses burst out to invade more cells, turn them into virus factories, and then destroy them.

In many cases, when a virus attacks, the victim's immune system can fight off the infection. Otherwise, huge numbers of people would die from colds and other minor illnesses. But still, sometimes the victim loses the fight.

No one knows where viruses came from. One theory is that they are scraps of rogue genetic material that somehow escaped from people, animals, plants, or bacteria. One researcher even suggested that viruses came from outer space, but most other scientists don't buy that idea. Whatever their origins, they are here to stay.

vicious, rapidly fatal diseases. But the illnesses start out in a pretty ordinary way, like many tropical diseases—like the flu, in fact—with a headache, fever, and aches and pains. Sometimes there's also a rash. Diarrhea and vomiting follow.

Then comes a truly awful symptom: about half the victims begin to bleed. They may vomit blood or pass it in their urine, or bleed under the skin or from their eyes, mouths, or other body openings. That's why the illnesses caused by Marburg and Ebola are called hemorrhagic fevers. The bleeding, though, is not usually what kills people; rather, most die because deep inside the body, fluids begin leaking out of their blood vessels, causing their blood pressure to plummet so low that a lack of blood flow causes failure of their heart, kidneys, liver, and other organs.

Although there are drugs that fight some viruses, there are none that can treat Marburg or Ebola. All hospitals can do is try to nurse people through the illness and keep them alive by giving them fluids and

Passengers on a flight from Hong Kong to Singapore attempt to protect themselves against SARS by wearing masks in 2003.

medicines to keep up their blood pressure and treat other infections that often set in on top of the virus. But in the countries where these viruses are most likely to originate, even the most basic forms of treatment may not be readily available.

In 2005, I traveled to Angola to report on the largest outbreak of Marburg fever ever recorded. It was my job to find out what was happening in a little-known region of Africa and to report on the international effort to fight a dreadful disease. There I saw firsthand the challenges that face doctors and aid workers dealing with epidemics in the third world, and the suffering inflicted on victims and their communities by one of the fiercest emerging viruses.

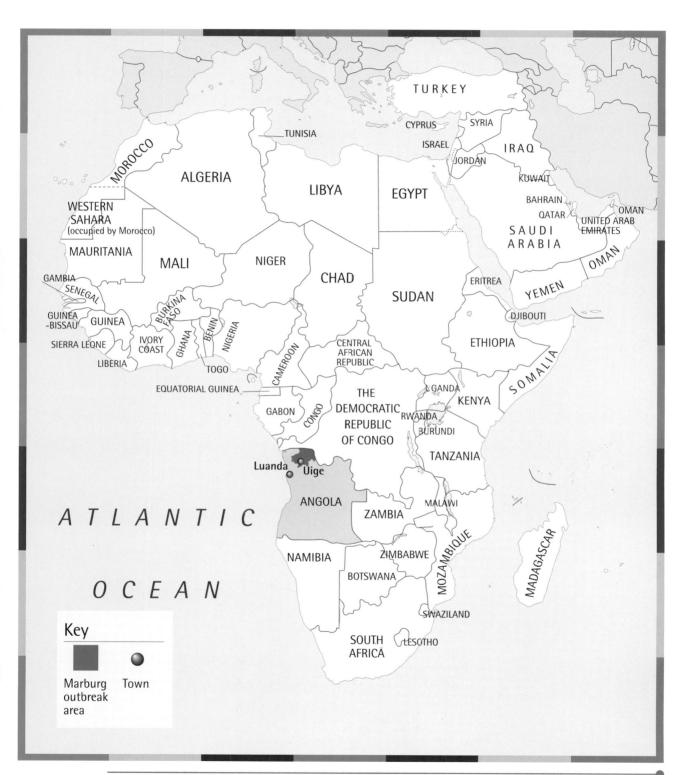

TURKEY
CYPRUS
SYRIA
ISRAEL
JORDAN
IRAQ
KUWAIT
BAHRAIN
QATAR
UNITED ARAB EMIRATES
OMAN
SAUDI ARABIA
OMAN
YEMEN

MOROCCO
ALGERIA
LIBYA
EGYPT
WESTERN SAHARA
(occupied by Morocco)
MAURITANIA
MALI
NIGER
CHAD
SUDAN
ERITREA
DJIBOUTI
GAMBIA
SENEGAL
GUINEA-BISSAU
GUINEA
BURKINA FASO
SIERRA LEONE
IVORY COAST
GHANA
BENIN
NIGERIA
LIBERIA
TOGO
EQUATORIAL GUINEA
CAMEROON
CENTRAL AFRICAN REPUBLIC
ETHIOPIA
SOMALIA
UGANDA
KENYA
GABON
CONGO
THE DEMOCRATIC REPUBLIC OF CONGO
RWANDA
BURUNDI
TANZANIA
Luanda
Uige
ANGOLA
ZAMBIA
MALAWI
NAMIBIA
ZIMBABWE
BOTSWANA
MOZAMBIQUE
MADAGASCAR
SWAZILAND
SOUTH AFRICA
LESOTHO

ATLANTIC

OCEAN

Key

Marburg outbreak area

Town

The Marburg
Story

Luanda, Angola

MONDAY, APRIL 11, 2005

Standing in a tent outside the Américo Boavida Hospital in Luanda, Angola, I peeled off my sweaty blouse and jeans and pulled on a green hospital scrub shirt and pants. It was noon, hot and humid—a typical day in southwestern Africa—and it felt as if there were no air in the tent. A rooster crowed from a field of weeds just outside, and as I tied the drawstring on my pants I thought, *I've been writing about medicine for twenty-five years, and I've never been to a hospital with roosters before.* The scrubs, not long off the clothesline, felt damp, and they reeked of bleach. But it was a reassuring smell. The tent had been pitched as a changing room for doctors and nurses just outside a building that housed the "hot zone," a special ward created for patients infected with the deadly, contagious Marburg virus. Bleach was the best way to kill the virus on clothing, equipment, and even people's hands.

It was my third day in Luanda, Angola's capital, a teeming city of four million where SUVs zigzagged around gaping potholes and women strode gracefully by with enormous baskets of bread or fruit balanced on their heads. About 180 miles (290 kilometers) north of us, the province of Uige (pronounced Weej) was in the grip of the world's largest epidemic ever of Marburg fever.

There is no cure for Marburg. By the time I arrived in Angola, of 214 people who had caught it, 194 had died, usually after being sick for only a week. It was a shockingly high death rate, among the worst for any infectious disease. Of the first 100 or so victims, many were babies and small children. The outbreak had taken Angola by surprise, and no one knew exactly how, where, or when it had started.

Although Marburg had first been identified in blood samples from patients in Uige in March of 2005, it had probably been killing people for months before that, maybe since October of 2004. Much of that time, doctors had probably been mistaking it for something else. There is so much disease in Africa—malaria, diarrheal infections, and yellow fever are just a few examples—that it is easy for a new illness to sneak in and gain a foothold. That is precisely what Marburg did: it blended in and got such a head start on doctors and health officials that suddenly, before they even knew what was happening, they had an epidemic on their hands. The disease was still spreading. Virus experts had flown in from all

Angola's capital, Luanda, is a bustling city of four million.

PATH OF A VIRUS

The Marburg virus does not naturally spread through the air. Some viruses do: measles, chickenpox, and influenza, for instance, can linger in the air even after a patient has left the room, and someone else who walks in later can be infected. Marburg is different: to contract it, a person must touch blood, vomit, urine, or other fluids from someone who is sick. A cough is dangerous only if the droplets hit someone else. And, fortunately, the disease does not usually make people cough. But the virus may live on surfaces, especially if it's got a puddle of blood or some other body fluid to lurk in, so people who touch contaminated objects can become infected if the virus finds its way into the eyes, nose, or mouth, or enters the bloodstream through a cut.

Once the virus gets into the body, it invades white blood cells and multiplies inside them, killing the cells or interfering with their function. Since white cells are essential to fighting off infections, the virus's attack on them may be part of what makes the disease so deadly. In Africa, doctors say, people who die of Marburg are often suffering from other infections as well. Whether those illnesses set in before or after Marburg is not always clear, but either way, the virus weakens the body's ability to fight back. On day three of the infection, a person might have as few as five viruses in a drop of blood. By day eight, there are five million per drop. Multiplied by the amount of blood in an adult's body, that works out to about six hundred billion viruses—just in the bloodstream.

"That's why dead bodies are kind of like bombs," said Dr. Heinz Feldmann, a virologist from the Public Health Agency of Canada, in Winnipeg, who set up a laboratory in Uige to test blood samples for Marburg.

The incubation period, the time between when a person is infected and when the symptoms show up, is estimated to be about three to ten days. The first symptoms are usually a headache, high fever, and aches and pains, followed by diarrhea and vomiting. There may be a rash. As the disease progresses, the virus invades the spleen, liver, and lymph nodes and then moves on into other tissues all over the body, including the skin and sweat glands. The disease interferes with blood clotting, and about half the victims hemorrhage. They may vomit blood and pass it in their urine, have hemorrhages under the skin and in their eyes and gums, and bleed from the nose and other body openings—all of which help the virus find its way into its next victim.

But it is a misconception that people bleed to death from Marburg, Dr. Feldmann said. Instead, they die from a type of shock that occurs when fluid leaks out of the blood vessels, causing blood pressure to drop. The leaking is caused by chemicals released from the millions upon millions of infected white blood cells.

over the world to try to stop it. Tomorrow, I would fly to the center of the outbreak, Uige.

From New York, where I work at *The New York Times*, I had been following reports from the World Health Organization about the epidemic in Angola, and urging (some might call it pestering) the paper to cover it. American newspapers were not writing much about the disease. Finally, when I sent around an e-mail noting that the outbreak had officially become the largest known Marburg epidemic ever, one of my editors said, "Do you want to go?"

"Sure," I said—and wondered immediately what I had volunteered for. But, I must admit, the disease fascinated me. I was a biology major in college, and the student in me wanted to know more. The reporter in me wanted to tell the story of the crisis in Angola.

A street vendor sells mangoes in Luanda.

Nearly half a million Angolans fled the country during its civil war, which claimed 500,000 lives. This family was among the refugees returning home in 2005, after a peace accord was signed.

Some people thought going there was a crazy idea. Colleagues, relatives, and friends asked if I wasn't afraid I would catch the disease myself.

Of course I was afraid. I would be walking into an epidemic of a contagious, incurable, and usually fatal disease, in an isolated part of a poor, crumbling nation with a shaky health-care system. At least one doctor and several nurses in Uige had caught the disease from their patients and died. The incubation period—the time between when a person is infected and when he or she becomes sick—is short, between three and ten days. I knew that if I became infected in Angola, I would probably die there, too.

But at the same time, I thought it should be possible to report on Marburg without catching it. Infected people aren't contagious until they start having symptoms, so I wouldn't have to worry around people who weren't sick. Even then, the virus does not spread through the air. To catch it, you have to touch body fluids like blood, vomit, and urine from sick patients. Many people in Angola became infected from taking care of others with the disease. Corpses, teeming with the virus, are especially dangerous, and some Angolans got sick and died from washing the body of a dead relative to prepare it for burial.

It seemed to me that if I didn't get close to sick people or dead bodies, and took care about where I went and what I touched, I should be able to avoid the virus. I would be interviewing experts in infectious disease, and I decided that I would follow their advice and do whatever they did to keep from being infected.

Still, there was a risk. The odds of not coming home were small, but real. Even without Marburg, Angola wasn't the safest place. It had been torn apart by civil war from 1975 to 2002, and the countryside was still littered with land mines, so there were many areas where you simply couldn't walk or ride. Outside Luanda, you weren't even supposed to drive up on the shoulder of the road to pass another car, because the shoulders had been planted with land mines. Medical care was poor, except in Luanda. Law and order were sketchy. The U.S. State Department Web site warned that bandits might stop cars along roads outside Luanda, especially at night, and that the police had been known to rob people. The State Department also said, "Police and military officials are sometimes undisciplined, and their authority should not be challenged." Even getting in and out of Angola could be tough, because there had been incidents in which officials at the airport pulled scams, detaining travelers or threatening to vaccinate them with unsterilized needles unless bribes were paid.

I booked flights and a hotel in Luanda, applied for a visa, and saw a doctor who specialized in travel medicine. He prescribed pills to prevent malaria and antibiotics to carry in case I got sick from tainted food. He also gave me five shots: vaccinations against polio, meningitis, hepatitis A, typhoid, and yellow fever. But there was nothing that could protect me from Marburg fever—except, perhaps, my own common sense.

I left New York on Thursday night, April 7. My arm was still sore from the shots. My suitcase was stuffed full of mosquito repellent, germ-killing hand cleaner, PowerBars, and packages of nuts in case I found myself in places with no food, or food I was afraid to eat. I was wearing a money belt hidden under my clothes, with about $4,000 in it. It made me nervous to carry so much money, but drivers and translators—the official language in Angola is Portuguese—would be expensive and would have to be paid in cash.

On the first leg of the trip, a flight to London, I sat next to a man who had traveled quite a bit in Africa.

"Fortunately," he said, "I've always been able to avoid Angola."

The Hot Zone

SATURDAY, APRIL 9, 2005

I arrived in Luanda on Saturday morning, checked into a hotel, and went to the World Health Organization (WHO) office. I would have preferred to walk there, but I took a taxi because I had been warned that crime in Luanda made it unsafe for visitors to walk in the streets.

The WHO, part of the United Nations, was bringing in doctors and other experts from all over the world to try to halt the epidemic. Each would stay for a short time and then be replaced. That first morning, I spoke with Dr. Dominique Legros, who had spent two weeks in Uige and was now on his way back to WHO headquarters in Geneva. His duties in Uige had included making daily visits to people who had had contact with Marburg victims, to see if they were coming down with the disease, too. He also responded to "alerts," reports of people who were sick with symptoms that might be Marburg. Of twenty alerts his team had checked out, half the patients had already died by the time they arrived.

Dr. Legros seemed tired and sad. He told me several things I knew I would keep in mind for the rest of my trip. To lower his risk of being exposed to the virus, he tried to avoid entering the homes of the people he was monitoring and instead spoke to them outdoors. He tried to stay

HALTING THE SPREAD OF DISEASE

Countries that suddenly find that they are dealing with epidemics or other health emergencies can get help from the World Health Organization, an agency of the United Nations that has 192 member countries. The health organization has a special branch—the Global Outbreak Alert and Response Network (GOARN)—that quickly dispatches international swat teams of doctors and other health experts to countries that ask for help in controlling epidemics. Some team members are WHO employees, but others are volunteers who venture into infectious disease "hot zones" like Uige without pay, to take care of the sick and in some cases to collect the dead.

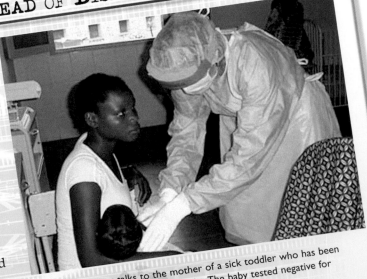

A WHO doctor talks to the mother of a sick toddler who has been in contact with a Marburg fever victim. The baby tested negative for the disease.

Teams began pouring into Angola in March almost immediately after the Marburg outbreak was recognized and Angola's Ministry of Health asked for help.

The United States agency that works most closely with the WHO is the federal Centers for Disease Control and Prevention (CDC). The CDC rotated several teams of infectious disease experts in and out of Uige during the outbreak, and sent one of its best public affairs officers, Dave Daigle, a tough but good-humored former army officer, to Uige to work for the WHO. It was Dave's job to deal with reporters who were clamoring for information about what was happening there. Scientists from the CDC and from Health Canada, a government agency, set up laboratories to perform blood tests that could tell within hours whether a sick patient was infected with Marburg. Doctors Without Borders, an international group based in France, sent doctors, nurses, and other experts to Uige to set up isolation wards to take care of patients, transport sick people to the units, and help safely remove the dead from their homes.

about one meter away from them and did not touch them. If he needed to check their eyes or look at their gums for hemorrhages he would ask them to pull down their lower eyelids or lips rather than doing it himself.

Finally, he said, it was important not to stay in Uige for too long. "If you do," he said, "you lose the necessary distance and you forget about the danger, which is always here, and you might put yourself in some sort of danger."

Two days later, I visited the Américo Boavida Hospital to learn how an isolation ward worked. Although the epidemic had begun in Uige, a few infected people had traveled from there and died in Luanda. Hospitals in Luanda were not equipped to take care of Marburg patients or to keep the virus from spreading to other patients or visitors. That was an ominous problem, since Luanda is a crowded city with an international airport that has flights departing for other cities in Africa and Europe. If people infected with the virus got on an airplane, they could carry Marburg around the world, in theory at least, because a person could be infected and yet still feel well enough to travel for anywhere from three to ten days before developing symptoms.

Doctors Without Borders, an aid group based in France, had set up a special ward only for patients with the Marburg virus, or with symptoms that might be caused by Marburg. An entire one-story clinic building that stood by itself at the back of the hospital grounds had been cleared out to create the ward. The idea was to keep people with Marburg separate from other patients. People who had suspicious symptoms would be kept in the isolation ward while their blood was being tested for the virus.

The doctors and nurses entered the isolation ward only after putting on protective gear that looked like a space suit, with masks, gloves, goggles, and boots, to ensure that they weren't exposed to the virus and couldn't accidentally carry it outside the hospital. Even though the hospital had flush toilets, a latrine had been dug in the ground behind the isolation ward to hold the patients' waste. It was safer to add bleach and bury the waste than to flush it, because if the plumbing ever got clogged, virus-laden waste could back up and infect other people.

That Monday, there was just one patient in the unit, a sixty-one-year-old man, Bonifacio Soloca. Admitted on Saturday, he was running a fever, and there had been blood in his urine and vomit. The bleeding could be a symptom of Marburg, but also of many other illnesses. Another hospital in Luanda had refused to admit him when his family had taken him there. Doctors considered him a likely Marburg victim because he'd been in another hospital where a patient died of Marburg. He could have been exposed to the virus there. Even so, his first blood test for Marburg had been negative. But the doctors wanted another test, just to make sure.

I arrived at the hospital early that afternoon with Evelyn Hockstein, a photographer based in Kenya. Dr. Benjamin Ip had just emerged from the isolation unit. His scrubs and his hair were sweat-soaked, his face still creased from the surgical masks and goggles he had recently taken off. Dr. Ip, a volunteer for Doctors Without Borders who normally works at an urgent care clinic in Las Vegas, said he had stayed with the patient for as long as he could, nearly two hours. But the ward had no air conditioning, and Dr. Ip was wearing so many layers of protective gear that he had started feeling overheated, dizzy, and faint. He had to come outside.

He was worried about his patient. "He's not good," Dr. Ip said, shaking his head. The patient could not eat or drink, even when Dr. Ip tried to feed him. He was so sick and weak that he could not get out of bed and had lost control of his bodily functions. When the doctors went in to see him, they often found him lying in his own waste and had to clean him and the room.

A hospital worker pours waste into a special latrine dug for the isolation ward.

If this had been a regular hospital ward instead of an isolation unit, Dr. Ip and nurses would have checked in on him often. But in the isolation unit they saw him only three times a day, for an hour or so each time. It

could take a half-hour or more just to put on all the gear, and almost as long to take it off properly, and people had to go into the unit in pairs in order to keep an eye on each other and make sure they made no mistakes that might expose them to the virus. Between those visits the patient was alone, without even a family member there to help him. Visitors were not allowed in the isolation unit, because it was thought to be too hard for them to put the gear on correctly, and too easy to take it off the wrong way and expose themselves to the virus.

The lack of visitors was a hardship for the patient; at many hospitals in Africa, meals aren't provided and there is little nursing care. Relatives are the ones who look after patients and bring them food. In this case, the patient's wife brought food to the hospital and left it for doctors and nurses to bring to him.

At first the doctors had asked the family to bring the food in plastic bags that could be thrown away, because nothing that goes into an isolation ward should come out again. But the family were upset by that suggestion.

"Plastic bags are humiliating in Angola," said Dr. Renato Souza, a Brazilian psychiatrist who works for Doctors Without Borders. "You put food for a dog in a plastic bag, not for a person."

The doctors and the family worked out a compromise: the food would be put into plastic bags, but the bags would be hidden inside a nice-looking box and taken out at the last minute. The first time he saw all the work the family had done to prepare the food and wrap the box in a beautiful embroidered cloth, Dr. Souza told me, he found himself close to tears. The family was suffering, he said, not just from worry about Mr. Soloca but also because they were being shunned by some of their neighbors, who were afraid of catching Marburg.

Though I was not allowed into the isolation ward, Dr. Ip agreed to show me how to put on the protective gear, the "space suit." That was how I wound up in the tent, changing into the green scrubs.

When I stepped out of the tent, he led me to the entryway of the building that housed the isolation unit, where a dressing area had been set up. Handwritten signs in Portuguese marked one set of doors as the entrance, *Entrada,* and the other as exit only, *Naõ entra aqui!* The entryway was divided by shelves full of gear to separate the people going in from the ones coming out. A strip of tape on the floor marked the line no one was allowed to cross without full protective gear. A door was propped open to let in some fresh air.

A couple of skinny cats darted in and out of the building. Couldn't they pick up the virus on their feet and spread it around? I asked. In theory, yes, they could, Dr. Ip said. They shouldn't be there. He had tried closing the door one night, but a cat got in anyway and then spent half the night howling to be let out. At that point, Dr. Ip gave up.

"If we didn't have cats, we'd have rats," he said, and shrugged. "This is Africa."

He found me a pair of heavy green rubber boots, also still damp and smelling of bleach. Then came more layers: latex gloves, disposable white coveralls with long sleeves, which had loops on the cuffs that slipped over your thumbs to keep the sleeves from riding up (I managed to put the coveralls on backwards the first time, and Dr. Ip politely managed to not laugh), a heavy rubber apron, a second pair of gloves, a surgical mask, a hood, a second mask, a pair of goggles like the ones people wear for skiing.

"Breathe only through your mouth," Dr. Ip said. "If you breathe through your nose you'll fog up the goggles."

His voice sounded muffled because of the hood I was wearing. I looked into a mirror, and the only part of myself I could see were my eyes behind the goggles. I looked like an astronaut or a mummy or a storm trooper from *Star Wars.* My breath was hot and damp inside the mask. I was sweating furiously and finding it hard to breathe. I felt as if I were wrapped in plastic, which I pretty much was. This was disgusting. How could anyone wear all this stuff in a hot place like Angola for more than five minutes, never mind actually work in it?

I couldn't wait to get out of the suit. But I couldn't just tear it off. I wanted to remove it exactly as the doctors did, and that meant following a strict set of directions, called a protocol. If you had been around the virus and removed the suit the wrong way, you could infect yourself. The idea was to get it off without letting your bare skin touch the outside, which might be contaminated. That meant peeling off one layer at a time in a certain way and in a certain order, with a helper standing by to remind you what to do and spray you with a bleach solution at certain steps.

Dr. Ip directed me. "Okay, now pretend I'm spraying you with bleach—*pssht, pssht, pssht,*" he said, aiming his imaginary sprayer at the boots, apron, and outer gloves. The apron came off first, then the boots. Then I unzipped the overalls and removed the outer gloves, which he told me to

The author tries on a biohazard suit with the help of Dr. Benjamin Ip . . .

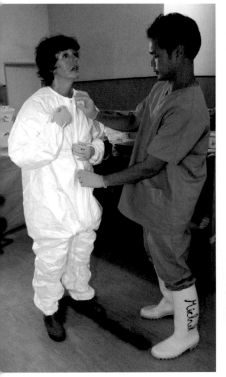
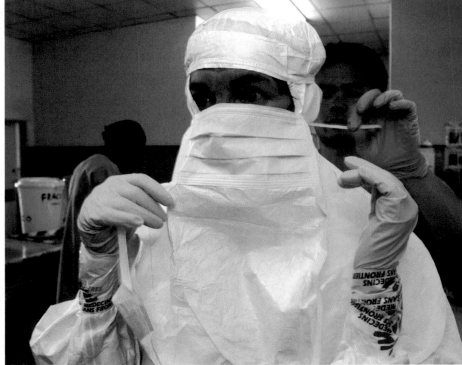

peel off inside out so that the outer layer would not be exposed anymore. I still had one pair of gloves on underneath. To take off the coveralls, I had to reach inside them without touching the outside layer and peel them off, again inside out. This was not easy. I blew it and touched the outside by mistake. Next I was supposed to take off the mask and goggles by pulling them forward, away from my face, and then up and over my head. I blew that, too.

"Oops, you touched your hair," Dr. Ip said. "If this were real we'd have to spray your head with bleach."

If it had been real, I would have contaminated myself several times over with the Marburg virus.

Fortunately it wasn't real, and I was out of the space suit. I'd had it on for just a few minutes, and already my green scrub shirt was soaked with sweat.

Before traveling to Angola, I had decided that if I found myself in a

... **and finds out** how difficult it is to remove it without "contaminating" herself.

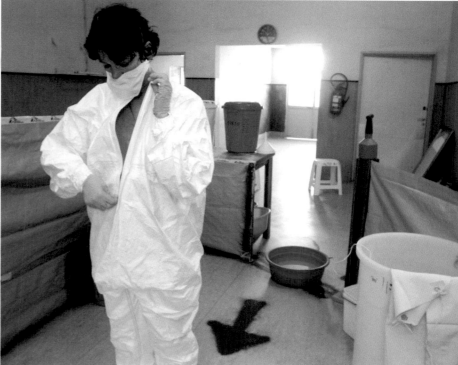

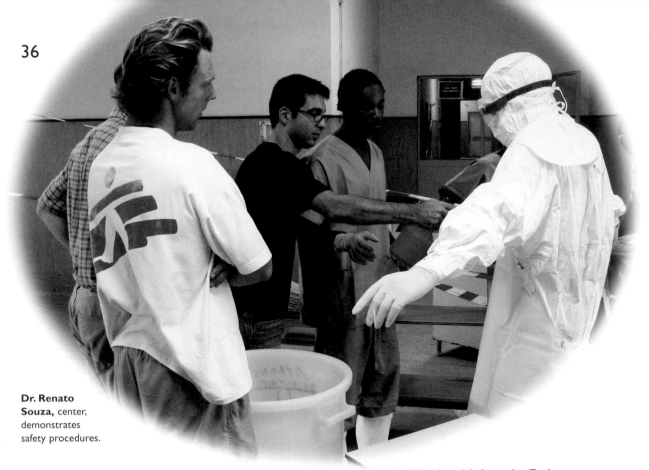

Dr. Renato Souza, center, demonstrates safety procedures.

place where I would need a suit to enter, I probably shouldn't go in. Trying the suit on convinced me that I was right. It would be too easy for an inexperienced person to make a mistake taking off one of the layers, and a mistake could be fatal. Even wearing a suit could be dangerous, because it might tempt me to go into risky places that I wasn't trained to handle. Without a suit I might miss out on some experiences, but the risk didn't seem worth it.

After I changed back into my clothes, a new shift of workers arrived to put on space suits and clean the ward. They were young men from Luanda who had been hired by Doctors Without Borders. It was a dirty, dangerous job, but they took it because their families needed the money. Some were still students.

As we stood in a shady spot under a tree, Dr. Souza talked with me about the cleaners.

When word went out that cleaning jobs were available, many young men had applied and gone through an introductory training session. Once they realized what the job involved, half left and never came back.

"We had to have six training sessions to get enough of them," Dr. Souza said. "But now I think we have a group that will stay."

Many of them decided to take the job when they realized that they would wear the exact same protective clothing as the doctors. That made them feel safe. But some said their mothers did not believe they would have the clothing and were reluctant to let them accept the jobs. So Dr. Souza snapped pictures of them in the suits to take home.

By late afternoon, it was time for the medical team to see the patient again. Evelyn shot pictures of Dr. Ip and his colleagues suiting up, and we stuck around so I could find out how the patient was doing and Evelyn could photograph the team members taking off their suits.

While we waited, Evelyn and I talked with some of the cleaners and a nurse, managing to get by with a crazy mixture of English, Evelyn's broken French, my broken Spanish, and the Angolans' Portuguese and few words of English. One of the cleaners, who went by his last name, Varela, said he was twenty-three and a hip-hop singer. He did some dance moves and introduced us to two other cleaners, who were also members of his hip-hop crew. They had given themselves an English name, The Lyrical Minds.

Suddenly, word came—from whom, we couldn't tell—that the patient had died. The doctors were still inside, so we couldn't be sure that it was true, but an awful quiet settled over everyone.

A moment later a woman approached the fence around the isolation unit and stood there quietly, waiting. She was carrying something. A guard spoke to her and then turned to me and put his hand to his mouth as if he were eating. My heart sank. She had to be the patient's wife, bringing him his dinner. She had no idea what we had just heard. I found Dr. Souza, and he hurried out to meet her and escort her into a large white tent that the doctors used to talk to patients' families in private.

Minutes later, Dr. Ip emerged from the isolation building, looking tired and sad. It was true. Mr. Soloca had died. He was dead by the time the doctors went in to check on him.

Now Dr. Ip wondered if they might have done more to save him. He said that earlier in the day he had considered starting an intravenous line to provide fluid and some nutrition but had decided against it.

"I don't know whether it would have made a difference," he said.

He had not started the line because it would have increased the nurses' and other workers' risk of being exposed to the patient's blood—and the virus, if he was infected—if they accidentally stuck themselves with a needle.

"It's a fine line to balance the care of the patient with the risk to yourself," Dr. Ip said.

It was Dr. Souza's job to explain to Mrs. Soloca that the family would not be allowed to claim the body or have the usual kind of funeral and burial. Since corpses were dangerous and could transmit the disease, Mr. Soloca would be buried by the government in a special cemetery picked for Marburg victims by Angola's Ministry of Health.

But one important custom would be honored. When someone dies in Angola, tradition dictates that the family see the person's face, to know for sure that their loved one is dead.

So, an hour or so after taking off one space suit, Dr. Ip put on another. In the dark, he and an assistant carried Mr. Soloca's body, which had been sprayed with bleach and zipped into two body bags, to a patch of bare dirt outside the isolation unit and set it down on the ground.

The bags were open just enough to reveal his face, and the doctor shone a flashlight on it. Mr. Soloca's wife and sons and his priest looked at him from the other side of a fence, wept, said a prayer, and left.

Later that night, as I packed a bag for the next day's trip to Uige, I kept seeing Mrs. Soloca in my mind's eye, patiently waiting with the dinner she had made for her husband, having no idea that he was already dead.

I thought of Mr. Soloca, spending his last days in an isolation ward and dying there, utterly alone. Once he was admitted, he never saw his wife and sons again. Did any of them expect that? Had they even had a chance to say goodbye? They were not allowed to visit, and Mr. Soloca almost certainly got less medical attention than he would have received if he had been on a normal ward, where doctors and nurses could easily check on him on the spur of the moment, without having to pile on layers of suffocating protective gear. Though no one could say for sure, I could not help wondering if he might have survived if only he had not been put into isolation. Whether Mr. Soloca had Marburg or not, he and his family were certainly victims of the epidemic and the fear it had created.

A week later I learned that the second blood test, like the first, was negative for the Marburg virus. Mr. Soloca was not infected. There had been no need to keep him in the isolation unit. What actually killed him was never determined.

Arrival in Uige

TUESDAY, APRIL 12, 2005

The pilot and the mechanic, both from South Africa, were yelling in Afrikaans. I don't know the language, but I understood the swear words anyway as they struggled to close the hatch on the tiny airplane that was supposed to fly us from Luanda to Uige. The plane, parked on the runway in the sun, was like an oven. The two men, the pilot inside and the mechanic outside, had been fighting with the door handle for more than an hour. Now, it was nearing five o'clock, and the pilot said that if they couldn't fix the door by then, we would not be able to fly to Uige that night. The sun would set at about six, and it would be too dark for him to fly back to Luanda. And no way was he going to spend the night in Uige.

This was not good news. Evelyn and I were eager to get to Uige and start working. Another reporter from *The New York Times*, Sharon LaFraniere, had gotten to Uige a few days ahead of us and was already filing stories. There was more reporting to do, and lots of pictures to take.

But we were stuck. There was no other plane to catch, no commercial flights to Uige. The only way to fly there was to hire a private plane and pilot, or to do what we were doing—catch a ride with the World Food Program, a program of the United Nations that flew food and medical supplies to Uige several times a week. It would take passengers for twenty-five dollars apiece, with a limit of about twenty-five pounds of baggage each (which, we quickly discovered, is not a lot).

Finally, with only minutes to spare, the door clunked shut. The pilot, tall and lanky, had to bend almost in half in the low cabin as he squeezed past us and folded himself into the cramped cockpit.

Within minutes we were in the air, flying north. Mile after mile of slums around Luanda were visible from the sky, shacks and shanties jammed together with no plumbing or electricity, and few real streets, just endless stretches of mud and ruts without a tree or a blade of grass. To the west, the South Atlantic glimmered all the way to the horizon. The city soon gave way to lush forests. It was nearly the end of the rainy season, but everything was still a brilliant green. For a moment I thought I'd like to explore that forest—until I remembered the ten million land mines in Angola.

Less than an hour later we landed in Uige. The airport, not much more than a landing strip, was on high ground, surrounded by fields of

World Health Organization epidemic specialists (in blue hats) visit a village in Uige, April 10, 2005.

tall grass. It had a view of rolling hills and valleys, palm trees, and, off in the distance, mud-brick houses set along winding red dirt roads. The elevation was about 2,700 feet (823 meters). It had rained recently, and the air felt cooler and fresher than in Luanda, which at its highest is only about 200 feet (61 meters) above sea level.

Uige is the name of both the province and its capital city. The province is big. It covers more than 22,000 square miles (56,890 square kilometers), nearly the size of West Virginia, and the Angolan government estimates its population at 800,000.

Sharon had hired local people as drivers and translators, and one of them picked Evelyn and me up. I tried my Spanish, hoping at least a few words would be enough like Portuguese for us to communicate. I was delighted to find it worked.

On the ride to our hotel, I saw that close up, Uige was not so lovely. It may once have been, but now, downtown, its pastel buildings were bullet-riddled and crumbling. Windows had been shot out and were screenless, and the streets were full of huge potholes. Empty lots were trash-strewn. Chickens pecked at the garbage.

Sharon had found rooms at a place called the Hotel Bunga, which she'd been told was the best hotel in Uige. It was a one-story building, similar to a motel in the United States, built in a U shape. The rooms opened onto a tiled veranda. Lizards scampered along the outside walls. The rooms were small and dingy, with just enough space for a bed and tiny night tables. My room had a row of pegs on one wall for hanging clothes. We spotted a cockroach the size of a hockey puck on one of Evelyn's walls. Fortunately, there was a mosquito net hanging from the ceiling that could be tucked in around the mattress at night. The sheets weren't dirty, but they weren't exactly clean, either. The towel in my room had a smell that could knock you out. And you wouldn't want to go barefoot on the floors.

Uige had no electricity, but the hotel had power for a few hours each day, when its private generator was running. The bathrooms were outside along the veranda, each to be shared by two guest rooms. No water came out of the showerheads. There were no sinks, and the toilets didn't flush. This was the kind of place where you would have to put used toilet paper in the trash, not the toilet. Uige must have had running water at one time, but it didn't now. The city had never recovered from all those years of civil war. There was a bucket of dirty-looking water that you were supposed to dump in the toilet to flush it, and a plastic barrel of less dirty-looking water for washing. You were guaranteed to get sick if you drank that water, I figured, but with luck it would be safe for washing. I hoped it was rainwater, because I figured that was more likely to be clean than water from a well or a stream. A shelf held a plastic pitcher and a basin so that you could wash by pouring the cold water on yourself over a hole in the cement floor that served as a drain.

A reporter from another publication had also been sent to Uige to write about Marburg. He called Sharon on her cell phone the day he arrived, complaining that he was in the filthiest, most disgusting hotel he'd ever seen in his life and he couldn't possibly stay there. Sharon told him our hotel wasn't great, either, but didn't sound as bad as his.

"Why don't you come here?" she suggested. "We're at the Hotel Bunga."

"I'm *at* the Hotel Bunga," he said.

That first night, I grabbed a book, a pair of glasses, and a flashlight, sprayed myself and the mosquito net with bug repellent, and crawled into bed under it, feeling like I was in a sort of mesh fortress. It was comfortable enough. I was awakened once during the night by what sounded like a mouse or rat scratching around in my room. I remembered what Dr. Ip had said: this is Africa. And I went back to sleep.

All in all, the Bunga didn't seem so bad. Sharon, Evelyn, and I had stayed in worse places. On the other hand, while the Marburg virus was fragile enough to be destroyed by hand washing, here we were, in the midst of an epidemic, in a city with no running water.

◆   ◆   ◆

To this day, no one knows exactly when, where, or how the Marburg virus first slipped into Uige. But doctors and nurses at the regional hospital there began to suspect that something was terribly wrong in October of 2004, when babies and children who had been brought to the hospital with seemingly treatable illnesses began mysteriously to die.

In November, the Angolan government sent blood samples to the Centers for Disease Control and Prevention in Atlanta, which tested them for several diseases, including Marburg. But the tests came back negative. No one knows why—the test for Marburg is considered very reliable. It is possible that the wrong people were tested, because doctors could not distinguish early cases of Marburg from more common illnesses like malaria. But it's also possible that Marburg really wasn't there at the time. There is no way to tell for sure.

But from October to the end of December, hospital workers said, ninety-five children died at the hospital—an alarming number even for Angola, where one child in four dies before the age of five.

In March, samples were sent again. This time they came back positive. And by then people were dying every day. That's when the World Health Organization, Doctors Without Borders, and the Centers for Disease Control and Prevention began sending in doctors, nurses, and scientists to try to stop the epidemic.

According to Dr. Matondo Alexandre, the former administrator of the provincial hospital in Uige, the outbreak may have started with a sick monkey. Children in Uige play with monkeys, he said, and people also kill monkeys and eat them. A person could be infected by contact with a sick monkey, or by touching raw meat from one.

Someone infected with Marburg who came to the hospital in Uige

MARIA BONINO

One of the first people to recognize that something was horribly wrong in the children's ward at the regional hospital in Uige, starting sometime in 2004, was Dr. Maria Bonino, a fifty-two-year-old pediatrician who worked there for an Italian aid group called Cuamm, or Doctors with Africa.

A colleague of hers, Dr. Enzo Pisani, an obstetrician, sat down with me one day in his office at the hospital to tell me about her.

She came from a family of doctors in Italy, and she had chosen to work as a pediatrician in Africa because the needs of children there were so much more urgent than those in Italy. She had worked in Africa for fifteen years, and she moved to Uige in 2003. She cared deeply about children and worked hard, and she knew a great deal about the tropical diseases that are rampant in Africa. She became a favorite of the nurses. More than most of the other doctors, she was a stickler for hygiene—hand washing and sterilizing equipment to prevent the spread of disease.

In 2004 and early 2005, she became increasingly worried about what was happening at the hospital.

"She sat across from me in that chair and said we were having too many strange deaths," Dr. Pisani recalled.

In a single day, she told him, she had taken care of four children who died with fevers and bleeding, from what seemed to be a hemorrhagic disease.

In March, right around the time that blood tests found Marburg in Uige, Dr. Bonino herself fell ill. She had malaria, which, like many people who live in Africa, she caught from time to time. But this time she did not recover as she usually did. The World Food Program flew her to Luanda, where she was hospitalized. Tests showed she had contracted Marburg. Looking back, Dr. Pisani thought she must have been infected on the day when she took care of those dying children; the incubation period fit. Her colleagues tried to find a way to get her back home to Italy. They even arranged for an airplane with a special isolation chamber so that she could fly without endangering the crew.

"But it was too late," Dr. Pisani said.

When a priest arrived to give her the last rites of the Catholic Church, a sacrament for people who are very ill or near death, Dr. Bonino tried to joke about what bad shape she must be in.

"But I think she knew," Dr. Pisani said.

She was buried in Luanda.

"I feel a tremendous sense of failure because she died," Dr. Pisani said. "We should have sent samples earlier."

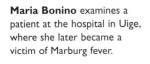

Maria Bonino examines a patient at the hospital in Uige, where she later became a victim of Marburg fever.

A **doctor** from the U.S. Centers for Disease Control takes a sample for testing from an Angolan woman who has had contact with family members who later died of Marburg.

could easily infect many others—doctors, nurses, and other patients—especially if the disease was not recognized.

Hospitals in developed countries have a lot of rules meant to prevent the spread of infection. Doctors and nurses are supposed to wash their hands and put on a fresh pair of disposable gloves before touching a patient. People thought to have contagious diseases are usually kept in rooms by themselves, and, if visitors are allowed, they may be asked to wear masks and gloves. Tubes and needles are disposable, and any equipment that is not disposable must be sterilized after each use.

But the picture can be quite different in developing countries that simply cannot afford all those precautions. Hospitals can become dangerous places if they are not equipped to isolate contagious patients and sterilize tools, and if they reuse disposable needles and other equipment that cannot be sterilized. Dr. Louis Ouedraogo, who works in Chad for the World Health Organization and who came to Angola to help stop the Marburg epidemic, told me that after decades of civil war, health care in Angola was in an "advanced state of dilapidation."

In poor countries, hospitals and needles may do as much to spread disease as they do to treat it. Without hospitals, clusters of diseases like Marburg and Ebola might die out quickly before becoming full-fledged epidemics, because the diseases are so deadly that patients and their families would probably get sick, quickly become bedridden, and die at home before they had a chance to pass the disease on to others outside the family.

But in the Uige hospital, children sometimes slept two to a crib or bed, and the beds weren't sterilized between one patient and the next— ideal conditions for spreading the virus.

In past Ebola outbreaks in other African nations, hospitals had acted almost like travel agents for the virus, helping it spread far and wide.

Patients wait for treatment outside the hospital in Uige.

In some hospitals, patients were admitted for malaria and then caught Ebola and died.

"Every time you have a hospital, you have amplification," said Dr. Pierre Rollin, a physician in the Special Pathogens branch of the Centers for Disease Control and Prevention.

It is not uncommon for disposable needles to be reused in developing countries, especially if they are the only means of giving a vaccination or other needed medicine. Vials of medicine that hold more than one dose become an added hazard when needles are reused, because inserting a dirty needle into the vial just once contaminates every dose.

"But what would you do?" asked Dr. Ouedraogo. He described the case of a desperately ill child who needs medicine—but the only way to give the treatment is with a used needle. "What would you do," he asked, "give that child a chance, or just sit there and pray?"

Hospitals in Africa are crowded, another ideal condition for spreading infections. And family members add to the congestion, since they must stay at the hospital to care for patients.

"You can have twenty-five people in one small room, with people sharing everything," Dr. Rollin said. "You can have a lot of contact, and transmission."

In addition to hospitals, many villages in Angola have traditional healers and small clinics that may reuse needles, and that send people home with needles and tubing to give themselves intravenous medicines at home. People in many developing countries like Angola expect to be given shots or intravenous treatments when they go to a doctor or healer; otherwise, they may not feel as if their treatment has been complete. Foreign doctors had a difficult job in Uige, coming in as outsiders and trying to explain to local people that their own customs could make them sick or even kill them. Tensions were inevitable, as I saw firsthand one morning.

Claudia's Funeral

WEDNESDAY, APRIL 13, 2005

The World Health Organization had set up a command post in a two-story building on a busy street in Uige. Every morning between nine and ten, medical teams, wearing knee-high rubber boots that could be disinfected with bleach, would pile into jeeps and vans and head out into the neighborhoods—*bairros*, in Portuguese—that surrounded the town.

The teams generally included two doctors and a few local people. The locals had been hired to help the doctors find their way and to introduce them to families in the *bairros* so that they would not be seen as outsiders who suddenly showed up and started poking around in people's business.

The teams' job was to check out "alerts"—reports of sick people who might have Marburg—or deaths, and to look in on people who had been in close contact with a Marburg victim. Anyone who might have been exposed to the disease had to be followed for twenty-one days to see if he or she got sick. If that happened, the teams would try to persuade that person to go to the hospital.

This kind of work, sometimes called "shoe-leather epidemiology"— finding every case, tracing every contact, going door-to-door, day after

day—is an essential part of every battle against an epidemic. I went with a team led by Dr. William Perea, from Colombia.

"This should be an easy day," he said. "No deaths, no alerts."

Then again, he said, no news might be bad news. The lack of reports might mean that people in Uige were hiding new cases or deaths from the foreign doctors.

Even though the medical teams were trying their best to help, some of the things they did, like taking sick people out of their homes and placing them in isolation units, had provoked intense anger and distrust in Uige. Nearly every patient died in the early days of the epidemic, so once they were taken into the hospital their families never saw them again. And when they died, the families were not allowed to claim the bodies, have funerals, or bury them in the usual way. Instead, the dead were quickly buried by soldiers.

To make matters worse, the people who took away the sick and collected the bodies and buried them were dressed from head to toe in protective gear, and it was white—a color associated with witches. Some people even suspected that the white-suited foreigners were somehow bringing the disease in with them.

People in Angola take witchcraft seriously. If I had any doubts about that, they ended in Uige when Sharon and I talked to a translator she had hired, a young math teacher named Ennis.

"Ennis, do you believe in witches?" Sharon asked.

"Oh, yes," he said instantly. "If a witch says you are going to die, you will die."

Health workers in Uige wearing protective gear. In Angola, the color white is associated with witches, which made the doctors in "space suits" especially frightening.

The day before I went out with Dr. Perea's team, people in one of the *bairros* had thrown rocks at another team's jeep. The week before, all the teams' trips had been halted for two days because of rock throwing by an angry crowd. Everyone was still tense about going into the *bairros*.

It took just a few minutes to drive out of town to an area of narrow, rutted red dirt roads winding among clusters of small mud-brick houses. Shirts were drying on clotheslines, children were playing outdoors, dogs were out wandering around. Everything looked so normal that it was hard to imagine a deadly disease lurking here.

Our first stop was the home of a man whose wife, a nurse, had died of Marburg. He was not ill. Standing outside his house, with curious neighbors looking on, he laced into the health team.

He demanded to know where the disease came from. Why didn't they just give him medicine, or a vaccine? When were they going to disinfect his house?

Dr. Perea told him that there was no vaccine, no medicine. All he and the team could do was find the sick and isolate them so they could not infect anybody else. Then the disease would be gone. They would come back to disinfect his house.

On our way to another stop, a message crackled across Dr. Perea's two-way radio: all teams back to headquarters. A van carrying another medical team had been attacked by a furious crowd that pounded on the vehicle with sticks.

Looking frustrated, Dr. Perea told the driver to turn around and return to headquarters.

For the time being, the World Health Organization was crossing off three *bairros* from the list its teams could visit. If anyone got sick or died in those areas, health officials would not know and would not be able to do anything to try to stop the disease from spreading. This was a real setback in their struggle to halt the epidemic.

I did not sleep well that night. I woke up in the middle of the night feeling awful, with a pounding headache that frightened me. Wasn't that the first symptom of Marburg? I lay under the mosquito netting thinking dreadful thoughts for a few moments until I realized I was being ridiculous: I hadn't done anything to expose myself to the virus.

And even if I had, I hadn't been in Uige long enough to develop symptoms. It had been a hot day, and I might have been a little dehydrated, which could cause a headache. And I realized my nose felt stuffed, and my throat scratchy. I was coming down with a cold. I drank some water and went back to sleep.

Sunday, April 17, 2005

Three space suits, three pairs of boots, a canister of bleach, and a body bag: the doctors loaded up the jeep and we all climbed in. It was Sunday morning, and we were going to a funeral. The medical team had offered to help prepare the body of a Marburg victim—to disinfect it with bleach and zip it into the heavy vinyl bag—so that the family could handle it safely and have a decent burial. Otherwise, soldiers would conduct the burial, and they had a reputation for tossing bodies into a hole in the ground and taking off as fast as they could, in terror of the disease. This was very upsetting to the families, because the custom in Angola is for the family to wash and dress the body of someone who has died, pray over it, and have a funeral that friends and relatives and neighbors can attend. Now people weren't even being given a chance to say goodbye.

The doctors wanted to help because they were sympathetic to the family. One member of the team, a virologist named Pierre Formenty, said he had seen one of those hasty, panicked burials by the soldiers. "It was disgusting," he said. "If it had been my wife I think I would have killed someone."

Funerals are important in Africa, and by helping people to carry out their traditions in a safe way, the doctors hoped to win some good will in Uige so that people would not be afraid of them and would not hide bodies or sick patients. "We can stop an outbreak like this in two or three weeks if the people trust and cooperate with us," Dr. Formenty said. "Otherwise it could be unending."

He continued, "We are fighting the battle of the disease. But first we have to win the battle of the heart, and the battle of the funeral."

We drove a short way from the downtown part of Uige, guided by Dr. Enzo Pisani, the doctor from Cuamm, who rode ahead of us on his Vespa motor scooter, helmetless and with his shirt partly unbuttoned in the heat. The streets quickly gave way to narrow, bumpy dirt roads that led into a village of small houses. Outside one, people were gathering.

Our driver stopped, and Dr. Formenty warned us all to stand at least a meter away from other people, even members of the team, as a safety precaution to avoid being exposed to the virus. A man stepped up and led us to a small yard behind a house where we could hear the sounds of hammering. Two men were putting the finishing touches on a coffin. It was rough wood, but skillfully crafted. And it was the smallest coffin I had ever seen. No coffin should be so small, I found myself thinking. Babies are not supposed to die. One of the doctors had tears in his eyes. I realized then that the man who had met our jeep was the baby's father.

Dr. Pisani knew the family, and as we walked back to the jeep he told me what had happened. The baby had died yesterday, one day after her first birthday. Her name was Claudia, pronounced "cloudy-ah." She had been sick for only a few days and had never had any bleeding, so the family did not suspect Marburg. But after she died a test for the virus came back positive. She had probably caught the disease from her mother, a nurse, who had most likely caught it from her patients. The mother had been ill for a week or so and seemed slowly to be recovering, Dr. Pisani said, and might even turn out to be one of the few Marburg survivors. But he still hoped to persuade her to go to the hospital. She lived with her husband and another daughter, and he did not know whether they were infected. And he said it was especially sad for this mother to lose her baby, because it had been difficult for her to have children and she would probably not be able to have any more. It was unbearable to think that she might infect her other child or her husband and lose them, too.

Meanwhile, the other three doctors were trying to solve a delicate problem. They had an adult-size body bag, not one meant for a child, and it seemed too big to fit into the tiny coffin. They stood in the road behind the jeep, sweating in the sun, turning the empty bag this way and that until they figured out a way to fold it to make it fit.

From inside the house we could hear people singing, wailing, and praying over Claudia's body. Dr. Pisani said the chanting had been going on all night, and he had been there for part of it. I was surprised: bodies were supposed to be highly contagious, and the other doctors would not even enter that house until they were covered from head to toe,

At the funeral of a Marburg victim in Uige, a coffin is disinfected before family members carry it to the gravesite.

complete with masks, goggles, and gloves taped to their wrists. But he knew the villagers and felt close to them. He had delivered many of their children. He didn't want to offend or hurt them by suddenly treating them as if they were contaminated. He encouraged me and the doctors to take a few minutes to join the neighbors who had gathered in a shady spot outside Claudia's family's house. I wondered to myself whether that was a good idea. I didn't know which of them had been inside the house, or whether anyone might be infected or contaminated with the virus. And yet it would seem rude to refuse. This was a baby's funeral.

Uneasy, feeling as though I were giving in to peer pressure to do something risky, I approached Claudia's house with the doctors. People smiled and offered us chairs. We sat. I noticed that our driver, an Angolan, stayed well away, on the far side of the jeep. I remembered what the doctor from the World Health Organization had told me on my first day in Angola: that it was best not to stay in Uige for too long, because the longer you stayed the more likely you would be to let your guard down, make a mistake, do something dangerous. Was I reaching that point?

After a few minutes someone told the doctors that the family was ready for them, and people streamed out of the house. We returned to the jeep and, as curious villagers watched, the doctors put on their space suits.

They entered the house single file, with the first one wearing the bleach canister strapped to his back, and spraying a path ahead of them as they went. Villagers looked in through the windows. "There is the mother," Dr. Pisani said, gesturing with his head toward a thin, listless-looking woman in a white blouse and a long skirt. He went to her, put his arm around her, leaned close and spoke to her. It seemed a very brave and kind thing to do, but also a dangerous one.

From inside the house I could hear the doctor who led the team shouting at one of his colleagues, swearing ferociously in French at the other man for making a mistake that could have contaminated the team. His voice was shrill, and I realized I was hearing not just anger, but also fear: even the experts were scared out of their wits by this disease.

After about twenty minutes the doctors emerged carrying the coffin, its rough wood now hidden by a neatly attached covering of pastel cloth. It had been sprayed with bleach.

They set the coffin on a table and went back into the house, dragging out mats, rugs, blankets, and other belongings. Anything that could not be disinfected would be burned.

The sky had darkened, and drops of rain began to fall as Claudia's father and another man, both wearing surgical gloves, placed the coffin into the back of a flatbed truck. Villagers piled in, the skies opened, and they headed for the cemetery in a driving rain.

The doctors took off the space suits, spraying each other with bleach as the various layers came off. They were soaked with sweat, and one turned his face to the sky and stood with his eyes closed, letting the rain wash over him. They sprayed their boots with bleach. I hoped they would offer to spray my sneakers, too, but they didn't, and I was too embarrassed to ask. It seemed foolish—I hadn't been in the house.

Dr. Pisani and I stood in the rain, talking. "One meter," Dr. Formenty said, scolding us for standing too close together. As I stepped back, Dr. Pisani told me that Claudia's mother was not the only infected person still living in the community. The night before, a pregnant woman, close to her delivery date and terribly ill, sought help at the maternity ward in Uige. Staff members there, suspecting Marburg, sent her to the isolation ward. Doctors drew her blood to test for the virus.

"She escaped," Dr. Pisani said. "After she was there for about an hour, a car drove up with four people in it, and they took her away. We tried to find her but we could not."

The test for Marburg was positive.

"I hope she dies before she has the baby," Dr. Pisani said, shaking his head sadly. Otherwise, he said, while giving birth "she could infect twenty people."

As he spoke, I found myself staring at his mouth, not wanting to believe what I was seeing. But there was no doubt.

"You're bleeding," I said. There was blood on his teeth; it seemed to be coming from his gums. He put his hand to his mouth and then looked at it. Blood. He shrugged.

The other doctors were ready to go. No one else had noticed that Dr. Pisani was bleeding. He climbed onto his Vespa and rode off through the rain. Soaking wet, the rest of us got into the jeep and drove back to Uige in silence.

After a funeral, a boy watches a bonfire built to burn items that had belonged to a Marburg victim.

The Outbreak Ends

TUESDAY, APRIL 19, 2005

After a week in Uige, it was time to go. The epidemic was still raging: with 266 people infected and 244 of them dead, there was no end in sight. But the work, day after day, was much the same—visiting contacts, checking out alerts, burying the dead. Sharon and I had written eight articles and had reached a point where we felt we might start repeating ourselves. Now we would track the outbreak as best we could from our home bases.

Evelyn and I got together with some other journalists to charter a plane to Luanda. Flying south from Uige, looking out over the forests, I wondered if the source of the virus lurked in there somewhere—and if it would ever be found.

Shortly after we landed in Luanda, I had a nosebleed. It started suddenly, for no apparent reason. It was scary, but I reminded myself that I did have a cold: my sinuses were blocked and during the flight I'd felt as if my nose might explode from the changes in cabin pressure. It couldn't be Marburg, I thought: people with Marburg got sick and ran a fever before the bleeding started. Apart from the cold, I wasn't the least bit sick and I hadn't been running a fever.

"Are you all right?" Evelyn asked, looking alarmed.

I said I was fine, and blamed the nosebleed on my head cold and the plane ride.

"Does that usually happen to you when you get colds?" she persisted.

"Yes," I said. That wasn't true. I hardly ever had nosebleeds. But I wanted her to stop asking. I wanted to stop thinking about it.

Before leaving Uige, I had mentioned Dr. Pisani's bleeding to Dave Daigle, the CDC public relations officer who was working there for the WHO. I had also mentioned it to one of the infectious disease doctors working on the outbreak. Both had promised to have doctors look in on Dr. Pisani.

I called Dave from Luanda. "Enzo's fine," he said. "They checked him out, and he's okay." He was badly in need of a dentist and he probably had gum disease, but he didn't have Marburg.

Neither did I. But even though I thought I was pretty calm about having been in Uige, I realized I was spooked by it after all, because when I got home I avoided hugging my family. I marked the date of Claudia's funeral on my calendar, counted it as the start of the ten-day incubation period for Marburg, and marked off the days until the time was up.

The next few weeks and months were frustrating for the doctors trying to snuff out the epidemic. In late April, a full month after the foreign medical teams had begun arriving in Uige, about three people were still dying every day. On April 29, the World Health Organization issued a scathing bulletin about the hospital in Uige, saying that practices there were still so sloppy that the hospital could prolong the epidemic and undermine all the hard work that had been done to try to stop it. Two doctors at the hospital had been exposed to blood from infected patients and were at risk of having been infected themselves. A baby died of Marburg, and as soon as the body was removed another child was put right into the same crib, without the crib's being disinfected. And the dead body of a Marburg victim was left out in an open ward, "uncleaned and uncollected," for more than eight hours, a potential source of infection for everyone nearby.

Stating that carelessness at the hospital could add weeks to the time it would take to control the outbreak, the report said, "Infection control procedures at the hospital have been seriously compromised."

That WHO report, as well as an article I wrote about it in *The New York Times,* sparked resentment from health officials in Angola, who did not want to be internationally embarrassed or criticized by the WHO or other outsiders. Publicity about Marburg had made soccer teams reluctant to compete in Angola, for fear that if players were injured and taken to an Angolan hospital they might catch Marburg there. The

Medical staff outside the hospital in Uige wait to disinfect the room of a Marburg victim once the body has been removed.

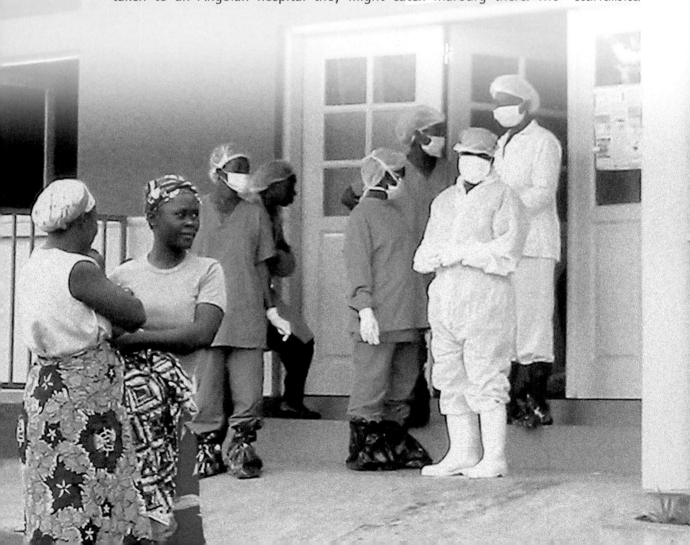

MAKING A VACCINE

Vaccines work by taking advantage of the body's natural ability to fight off diseases. With many viruses, like chickenpox and measles, for instance, people who catch the diseases once become immune and never catch them again. That protection occurs because the body has powerful defenses, an immune system consisting of a network of fighting cells and proteins that can neutralize germs. The immune system fights off the germs and also remembers the ones it has been exposed to so that it can attack them if they try to invade again. What generally sets off the immune response is some protein on the outside of a germ that the system recognizes as foreign—an invader.

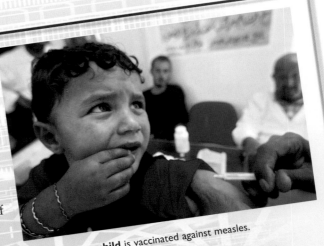

A Palestinian child is vaccinated against measles.

In a sense, vaccines trick the immune system into thinking the body has been invaded, so that it will be prepared to fight off a particular germ before an infection can take hold. Sometimes, as in the case of the polio vaccine, a dead or weakened form of the virus will be enough to do the trick. Other vaccines may contain just the proteins that trigger the immune response.

In the case of the new Marburg and Ebola vaccines, the scientists used another virus, called VSV, for vesicular stomatitis virus, which causes a mouth disease in cattle but rarely infects people. They chose it because it has a similar genetic structure to the Marburg and Ebola viruses, and because other researchers had used it successfully in developing vaccines.

They altered VSV by removing one of its genes—the change makes it harmless— and replacing it with a gene from either the Marburg or Ebola virus. The transplanted gene forced VSV to produce Marburg or Ebola proteins on its surface. The proteins cannot cause illness, but they provoked an immune response that protected monkeys in their study.

government did not want to miss out on sports matches because other countries were afraid to play in Angola.

After the bitter reaction to the report about the hospital errors, bulletins from the WHO became brief and bland, and it became harder to figure out what was really going on.

But there was good news on a different front. In June 2005, researchers from Canada and the United States reported that they had created vaccines that could prevent Ebola and Marburg in monkeys. Successfully immunizing monkeys is an essential step toward making vaccines for people.

Monkeys given just one shot of the new Marburg or Ebola vaccine and later injected with a high dose of the virus didn't even get sick, whereas normally they would die. A later experiment, reported in April 2006, had an even better outcome: it showed that Marburg vaccine works even if given *after* monkeys were exposed to the virus.

The vaccine work had started years before—not so much out of concern for Africans, but because governments and the military in developed countries like the United States became afraid that Marburg and Ebola could be made into weapons that would be used against them. That fear of bioterrorism arose during the 1990s after a scientist who had defected from the former Soviet Union said that Russian scientists had stockpiled the Marburg virus and packed it into warheads for possible attacks on cities or battlefields.

It will be a few years before the new vaccines are ready even to be tested in humans, and if they prove successful it will still be five or six years before they are ready to come on the market.

Even then they won't be used for routine vaccinations. They are meant to be given to health workers in high-risk areas, to researchers who work with the viruses, and to people who have been exposed to the disease, like relatives of sick patients. But it is not clear if the vaccines will be available or affordable in desperately poor African countries like Angola, where they are needed most.

By July, the epidemic in Uige seemed to be slowing down. The last known death from Marburg occurred on July 21, 2005. According to the World Health Organization, there were a total of 374 cases and 329 deaths; the fatality rate—the percentage, out of the people who contracted the disease, who died—was 88 percent. In late August, a report posted on the Web site of a medical society specializing in infectious disease said, "The outbreak can be considered to be virtually at an end. Attention can perhaps turn now to investigation of the sources of the outbreak."

Indeed, common sense would say that to prevent another Marburg outbreak in Angola or elsewhere, it would be a good idea to figure out how this one began, as well as how it got such a running start on medical experts. Virus samples taken from various patients were all the same, indicating that the virus had been introduced into the population just once from a single source and had then spread from person to person. But, so far, no investigation to find that source has taken place. And, when I spoke to Pierre Rollin and Tom Ksiasek, two CDC scientists who had traveled to Angola during the outbreak, they said it seemed unlikely that a hunt for the source of the epidemic would ever happen. There was so much confusion about when and where the epidemic started that it might well be impossible to pick up the trail.

"Do you know when the outbreak started?" Dr. Ksiasek asked. "I don't."

Angola's epidemic of Marburg fever, the largest ever in the world, seems to be over. But the virus is almost certainly still lurking somewhere in Africa, and there is no way of knowing if, when, or where it will mysteriously emerge again.

Animal Origins

I t's most likely that the Marburg fever outbreak began with an animal. Many emerging diseases start out in animals and somehow "jump species" to humans.

Sometimes the animals that spread these viruses to people get sick, too. In monkeys and apes, for instance, the death rates from Marburg and Ebola are even higher than in humans. West Nile disease kills many birds, and so does bird flu.

But viruses often have what scientists call a natural host, or reservoir—an animal that can carry the virus for long periods of time without being killed by it. If there were no natural host—if every infected animal got sick and died—viruses would probably die out, too. So scientists reason that between epidemics many deadly viruses lurk somewhere in nature, in an animal that has evolved together with the virus over millions of years and is not bothered by it. Epidemics may be accidents that occur when the virus jumps into some other species, some innocent bystander that has had no time to adapt to the virus, but stumbled into its path and cannot cope.

What suddenly brings people into contact with insects or animals? Why exactly does a new disease emerge? And once it gets into people, how do they spread it to one another?

War is one of the factors associated with the spread of disease.

In a 2000 report, the World Health Organization identified a long list of factors that could play a part. They included climate change and also forces that might cause people or animals to move into new areas, bringing them together and exposing people to new diseases—things like population growth, migration, war, and travel. Once a disease finds its way into people, they may then spread it to one another through sex, intravenous drug use, food, organ transplants, and breakdowns in public health measures like sanitation, vaccination, and insect control.

For instance, researchers say that global warming may be contributing to the warm winters and summer droughts that seem to favor the spread of the West Nile virus.

Dr. Paul R. Epstein, associate director of the Center for Health and the Global Environment at Harvard Medical School, says an important consequence of warming can be an increase in "extreme weather events" —droughts punctuated by torrential rains. Drought, he said, increases populations of the mosquito species *Culex pipiens,* which plays a major role in spreading West Nile virus among birds and from birds to people.

He says drought might also wipe out dragonflies and amphibians, which destroy mosquitoes. Drought may also aid the spread of infection by drawing thirsty birds to the pools and puddles where mosquitoes breed. "Hot weather plays a role, too," Dr. Epstein said. "Warmth increases the rate at which pathogens [disease-causing agents like viruses and bacteria] mature inside mosquitoes."

Climate is not the only factor. As wilderness is developed and animals' specialized habitats are destroyed, creatures like rats and crows often take over. Known as generalists or opportunists, animals that thrive near developed areas tend to be hardy species that can eat almost anything and live almost anywhere. If, like crows, they also happen to be capable of carrying a germ like the West Nile virus and spreading it through mosquitoes to people, they become an important source of outbreaks.

Human activity is believed to have played an essential role in the birth of the AIDS epidemic. Research has shown that the virus was originally a chimpanzee virus—simian immunodeficiency virus, or SIV— and scientists think it jumped species into humans who were exposed to infected blood while hunting and butchering chimpanzees for food or for sale as "bush meat." People then began spreading it to one another through sexual activity or blood transfusions, or by sharing needles used to inject drugs.

There are many SIVs, and some researchers say that they fear that others may also make the jump into people. Such a jump could be disastrous, leading to another contagious AIDS-like infection in people—one that could not be detected by current blood tests.

The scientists' concern stems from an enormous expansion in Africa of the bush-meat trade. It has grown in part because logging roads have opened up remote regions for hunting and shipping of the animal carcasses. Researchers have found surprisingly high rates of SIV infection in meat taken from primates in bush-meat markets in Cameroon.

In May 2002, a team from the United States, Cameroon, France, and Belgium reported that members had screened more than seven hundred primate carcasses and found SIV infection in 20 percent of them. More than thirty primate species were known to carry strains of SIV.

Dr. Beatrice Hahn, a professor of medicine at the University of Alabama at Birmingham and a member of the team, said: "Three things were surprising: the rate of infection, the diversity of viruses, and the amount of bush-meat hunting that was going on. It shows for the

A pygmy hunter-gatherer takes aim with his crossbow in a forest in Cameroon. Eating and handling dead monkeys could cause SIV to leap to humans.

Chimpanzees can carry SIV, the virus suspected of mutating to become HIV.

first time that there is no doubt that humans are routinely exposed to a wide variety of viruses from this activity. We suspect some may have already jumped."

If such a jump has already occurred, that means that people may be carrying potentially dangerous viruses, and may pose a threat to the blood supply. New, unidentified viruses could slip undetected past current blood tests. And since blood from a single donor could potentially be transfused into multiple recipients, one undetected case of an emerging virus could spread quickly through blood banks. Dr. Hahn said: "You do not want to transfuse the blood of a person who might have gotten such an infection. You don't have to be freaked out or a doomsday monger, but I think it would be a mistake to ignore it."

Indeed, recent history indicates that it is a mistake to ignore the signs that any virus is finding its way to new regions or hosts it has not infected before. "Local" outbreaks can spread far beyond their origins with surprising speed.

Marburg fever, avian flu, HIV, SARS, monkeypox, West Nile disease, and hantavirus are all caused by viruses that made the leap from animals to humans in recent decades. The stories of their emergence show a pattern: some activity brings the first human victim in contact with an infected animal or mosquito. What happens next—whether the virus sweeps the globe or is confined to a local outbreak—depends on a number of factors, including the contagiousness of the virus, how it is spread, how quickly the new disease is detected, and the availability of treatments or preventatives.

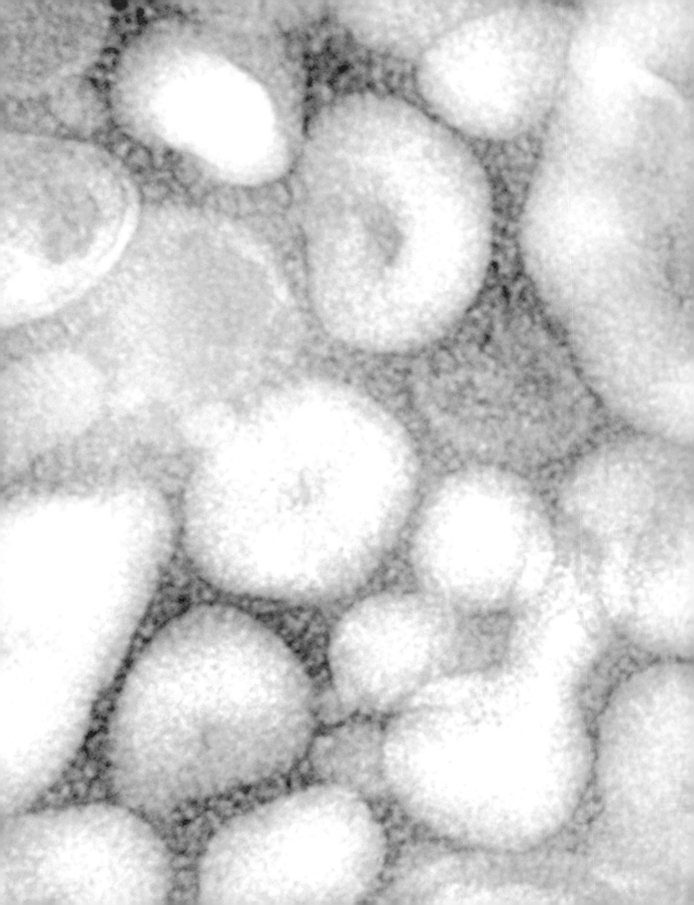

Seven Deadly Diseases

```
Marburg Fever
First recognized: 1967
Region of origin: Africa
Host animal: Carried by primates;
reservoir unknown, bat suspected
Virus family: Filoviruses
Number of cases (Angola, 2005): 374
Number of deaths: 329
Outlook for the future: Uncertain. Could
emerge again, but a vaccine, successful in
primates, may also protect humans.
```

Out of Nowhere

Before 1967, doctors had never heard of the disease caused by the Marburg virus. The illness erupted that year in several cities in Europe—Marburg and Frankfurt, in Germany, and Belgrade, Yugoslavia—when people suddenly came down with a mysterious ailment that started with fever and aches and pains and ended, dreadfully, with bleeding. Relatives and health workers caught the disease from the first victims. In all, thirty-one people got sick and seven died. A new virus was discovered in blood samples from patients, and, in keeping with tradition in the world of virus research, it was named for the place in which it was first found—Marburg.

But where had it come from? How could a deadly new virus suddenly pop up, as if out of nowhere?

Scientists made an intriguing and alarming discovery. The first victims worked in laboratories, doing medical research that involved monkeys. All had handled green monkeys from Uganda, in east-central Africa. Some of the monkeys had been sick and had died, but it didn't occur to anyone that whatever had killed them might spread to humans—not until people became desperately ill. And by then, it was too late.

It's a mystery where the Marburg virus lurks between outbreaks. It must have a natural host in some animal, but which animal is not known for either Marburg or its cousin, the Ebola virus. Ebola outbreaks have occurred in people eating meat from monkeys and chimps, and health authorities in Africa warn people there to stay far away from the corpses of dead primates, because they may have died of Ebola and be infected with the virus. (Cooked meat is probably not harmful, but people who handle the raw meat can become infected.) Scientists have ruled out monkeys and apes as the reservoir for these diseases, because the death rates of these animals if they contract Marburg and Ebola are even higher than those of infected people.

Several Marburg victims in South Africa and Kenya had recently visited caves. And in an outbreak that killed 128 people in the Democratic Republic of Congo from 1998 to 2000, nearly all the victims were miners. The link to caves and mines has led scientists to suspect that bats carry the virus. Two victims had recently visited Kitum Cave in Mount Elgon National Park in Kenya. The cave is full of bats and awash in their droppings, called guano.

Green monkeys (also known as vervet monkeys) were linked to the first documented outbreak of Marburg fever in Germany.

Dr. Douglas Bausch, an expert in hemorrhagic fevers at Tulane, who studied the Congo outbreak, said that before the connection to mines was made, one research group had suggested that elephants might carry Marburg.

"Having not seen any elephants enter mines there, I think we can exclude elephants," he said.

"The candidate that always interests us is the bat," Dr. Bausch said.

According to Dr. Bausch, the mine in Congo was full of bats of many species. And laboratory studies by another researcher, in South Africa, found that bats could carry the virus for long periods without getting sick. Workers in a mine could easily

BEWARE OF BATS

Bats are fascinating creatures, and play an important part in many ecosystems. But some species of bats are known to carry deadly viral diseases that can spread to people, and are suspected reservoirs for others:

⚠ Severe acute respiratory syndrome (SARS)
⚠ Nipah virus encephalitis
⚠ Rabies
⚠ Marburg hemorrhagic fever (suspected)
⚠ Hendra virus encephalitis
⚠ Ebola hemorrhagic fever (suspected)

African bats in a cave in Congo.

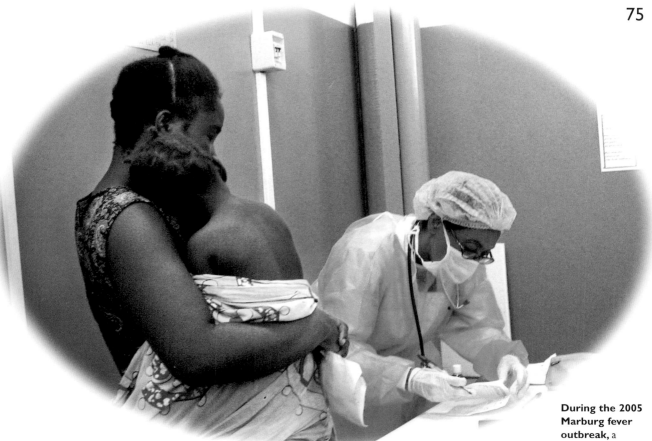

During the 2005 Marburg fever outbreak, a woman brings her child to be tested at the David Bernardino hospital in Luanda, April 4, 2005.

come in contact with virus-laden droppings by touching floors or walls in the mine, and then touch their eyes or mouths and infect themselves, Dr. Bausch said.

Researchers captured and tested about five hundred bats from the mine and never found the Marburg virus. However, there were literally millions of bats in the mine, and entire species probably went untested. Sometimes only one species will be the principal carrier of a particular virus. The scientists may simply have tested the wrong ones.

Another aspect of the Congo outbreak points to bats, or perhaps some other creature that inhabits mines and caves: the epidemic stopped when the mine became flooded and no one could enter it anymore. But there are no mines or big caves around Uige. Where the virus in Angola came from is still a mystery.

Avian Flu-H5N1
First recognized: 1997
Region of origin: Southern China
Host animal: Aquatic birds
Virus family: Influenza viruses
Number of cases: 205 by spring 2006
Number of deaths: 113 by spring 2006
Outlook for the future: Uncertain. A pandemic
is possible but not inevitable.

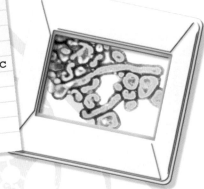

The Possible Pandemic

A lot of people think of the flu (short for influenza) as a minor illness or just a bad cold, and tend to call any mild ailment the flu. But real influenza, caused by a specific group of viruses, can actually be a dangerous illness, and it's a mistake to underestimate it.

According to the Centers for Disease Control and Prevention, every year in the United States, 5 to 20 percent of the population gets the flu, more than 200,000 people are hospitalized from its complications, and 36,000 die. And that's in an average year, not one of a pandemic. Young children, people over sixty-five, and those with chronic illnesses like asthma have the greatest risk of complications and death from the flu.

Pandemics occur when a new flu virus emerges. That happens when an existing virus suddenly changes so dramatically from previous strains that people have never encountered anything like it before, so they have no immunity to it.

Flu viruses are changing all the time, but in small ways. The big changes that can lead to a pandemic are much less common. Called an "antigenic shift," such a change usually occurs when different flu viruses mix in some animal or human host and swap genetic material to produce a new virus. If the new virus is virulent (meaning it can make people sick) and spreads easily from person to person, vast numbers will catch it and become extremely ill. The rates of illness and death will be much higher than with an ordinary flu.

Only influenza viruses that belong to a group called Type A can make antigenic shifts and cause pandemics. Wild birds in Asia are thought to be the world's main source of Type A flu viruses. They transmit the disease to domestic birds like chickens. In China and other Asian countries, many people live in close quarters with chickens, ducks, and pigs, and flu viruses from birds and mammals can mix to create new strains capable of infecting people.

In the twentieth century there were three pandemics, in 1918, 1957, and 1968. All were caused by Type A viruses. According to the CDC, the 1957 and 1968 pandemics were caused by viruses containing a combination of genes from a human flu virus and a bird flu virus. The 1918 pandemic virus appears to have been strictly a bird flu that somehow managed to jump species to people.

The 1918 pandemic—called the Spanish flu—was the worst one by far, killing fifty million people worldwide. No one who lived through it ever forgot it. My mother, who was born in 1911 and grew up in New York City, said her mother sent her to school with a string of mothballs around her neck, thinking they would somehow keep the flu away.

Many scientists believe that based on history and timing alone, the world is overdue for another pandemic. Since 1997, scientists and health officials all over the world have been increasingly worried that a bird flu (also called avian flu) found in that year could erupt into the next pandemic. It is a Type A virus, and its subtype is H5N1, which is a sort of code referring to proteins on the surface of the virus that set it apart

Migrating birds have carried H5N1 across continents and international borders.

from other Type A viruses.

What alarms scientists about this virus is that, although it was initially thought to infect only poultry, it suddenly jumped from birds into people—and turned out to be quite deadly in humans. This jump happens only occasionally, but when it first occurred in Hong Kong in 1997, eighteen people got sick and six died. Hoping to stamp out the virus, the government in Hong Kong destroyed the country's entire poultry industry—more than a million birds—in just a few days, and disinfected its markets. Buddhist monks and nuns in Hong Kong prayed and meditated for the souls of the slaughtered chickens, and world health officials praised Hong Kong for averting what might have turned into a pandemic.

But H5N1 persisted in other parts of Asia, particularly China's southern Guangdong province (which also gave rise to another deadly viral disease, SARS). Some wild water birds may be natural hosts for it, capable of spreading it far and wide during migration. Now it seems to be spreading to more and more bird species and has infected cats and pigs.

The persistence also worries scientists, because most bird flus emerge briefly, do not spread too far, and then vanish. This one won't go away.

"You get this compounding sense of risks," said Dr. Bruce Gellin, director of the National Vaccine Program Office. "First it's in some birds. Then more. Then more area, then more mammals, and then to humans, albeit inefficiently."

H5N1 has killed millions of birds in Asia—it is nearly 100 percent fatal in chickens—and has prompted governments to slaughter entire flocks to try to keep it from spreading. But it no longer seems possible to contain the virus. By late 2005, it had found its way to Europe. It soon reached Africa, and is expected to continue to spread. Of the first 200 or so human victims, about half died. It is impossible to say what the true death rate is, because it is not known whether some infected people have no symptoms or just mild ones that health officials never hear about. But if the disease does turn out to kill half its victims, or even a quarter of them, that would be an alarmingly high death rate. Even 10 percent would take an enormous toll. By comparison, even though the 1918 pandemic killed fifty million people, they made up less than 5 percent of those who were infected.

The alarm about avian flu heightened in October of 2005 when a scientific team reported that the 1918 flu virus also appeared to have been a bird flu that jumped directly to humans.

The main reason H5N1 hasn't caused a pandemic already is that it does not seem to spread from person to person. So far there are only a few cases in which people may have infected each other. Generally humans catch it from birds but then do not spread it. The 1918 flu, on the other hand, was highly contagious.

All H5N1 needs to do to become a pandemic virus, Dr. Gellin said, is "become an efficient transmitter among humans."

But no one knows if that will ever happen.

Dr. Edwin Kilbourne, an expert on flu viruses from New York Medical College, said fears of avian flu were exaggerated. In his opinion, many people will have some immunity to it because it is distantly related to earlier forms of flu to which they've been exposed. In addition, he said, if avian flu does become more contagious, it will probably become less lethal. That should occur simply because the most contagious viruses are the ones that do not kill their hosts right away but let them stay alive to pass the disease on to others. Deadlier strains are more likely to die off when their hosts do, before transmission can take place.

In 2005, government scientists in the United States announced that they had created a vaccine that would protect people against H5N1. But that vaccine must be given in very high doses to work in even half of the people who get it, meaning that enormous amounts will be needed. Other teams are also working on vaccines. But it is not clear when a vaccine will become available, or whether it will be possible to make enough to protect all the people who will need it—if it ever becomes necessary.

Most scientists believe that someday, whether it is H5N1 or a different virus, there will be another flu pandemic.

"You have to prepare for the worst-case scenario," said Dr. Anthony Fauci, director of the National Institute of Allergy and Infectious Diseases. "To do anything less would be irresponsible."

HIV and AIDS
First recognized: 1981
Region of origin: Africa
Host animal: Probably chimpanzees
Virus family: Retroviruses
Number of cases: Forty million now infected
Number of deaths: Twenty million so far
Outlook for the future: Desperate. No vaccine
yet; drugs to control the disease not
widely available in the hardest-hit
developing countries.

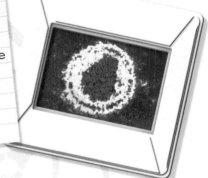

"Five Previously Healthy Individuals"

If you are in your teens or early twenties, you probably grew up knowing about AIDS, the acquired immune deficiency syndrome. But thirty years ago, no one had heard of AIDS. For all intents and purposes it didn't exist. It may be hard to imagine a world without AIDS, but earlier generations couldn't have imagined a world with it. If someone had described a disease like AIDS, people would have thought it was science fiction. They couldn't see the catastrophe heading their way, even as it began to unfold.

"*Pneumocystis* Pneumonia—Los Angeles" was the heading on a brief article published on June 5, 1981, by the Centers for Disease Control and Prevention in its bulletin, the *Morbidity and Mortality Weekly Report.* The article described "five previously healthy individuals," young men ages twenty-nine to thirty-six, treated at three different hospitals for an unusual type of pneumonia caused by the bacteria *Pneumocystis carinii.* The men had other infections as well, like fungal infections in their mouths and throats. Two died, just a few months after they first fell ill.

What caught doctors' attention about those cases was that

healthy people do not normally catch *Pneumocystis pneumonia*; it is an "opportunistic infection," meaning it takes advantage of patients who cannot fight back, who have something very wrong with their immune systems and lack the normal ability to shake off infections. Fungal infections in the mouth are often opportunistic as well.

The report also noted that all five men were homosexual, and said their illnesses might have had something to do with their lifestyles or might be a "disease acquired through sexual contact."

Concise, blunt, and carefully written, that article turned out to be the first published description of the illness that later came to be known as AIDS. The weekly publication that carried the report was a five-by-eight-inch booklet the size of a theater program, and copies of that little journal became historic documents in the world of infectious diseases, as famous as the Declaration of Independence or the Constitution.

But at the time, few could have imagined that those five cases were signs of a worldwide epidemic that would eventually kill more than twenty million people, and which currently infects forty million, the vast majority of them in southern Africa. In that part of the world, AIDS has killed vast numbers of young adults, wiping out work forces and making orphans of millions of children.

The birth of AIDS was the end of innocence for a society that was still squeamish about many things sexual, especially homosexuality and sexually transmitted diseases. It was also a rude awakening for a scientific world that smugly believed all infectious diseases had been discovered and would soon be conquered by the wonders of modern medicine. More than any other single disease, AIDS made scientists face the reality that new infectious diseases could emerge anytime, anywhere, without warning.

By the time the 1981 report came out, the new disease had already started sweeping through gay male populations in New York and San Francisco, killing most with frightening speed and causing horrific illnesses along the way, even some types of cancer. It was almost beyond comprehension. On a reporting trip to a hospital in San Francisco in the early 1980s, I met one young man after another, all going blind from a virus that was attacking their retinas, the layer of cells at the back of the eye that respond to light. Doctors couldn't explain why it was happening.

Like most reporters, I'm a bit of a pack rat when it comes to saving my notes and the phone numbers of people I've interviewed, in case I want to call them again for future articles. But in the early days of the AIDS epidemic, I quickly learned that most of the patients I talked to would not be around for the next article.

At first, theories abounded. The disease was initially called GRID, for "gay-related immune deficiency," and some doctors thought it was related to drug use, exposure to semen, or a certain combination of germs picked up from multiple sexual partners. Some predicted the disease would never be a major threat for anyone but gay men.

In 1983 researchers found the cause of AIDS, a virus that they named the human immunodeficiency virus, or HIV.

It soon became clear that AIDS was not just a disease of gay men. In the United States they just happened to be the first to contract it. The virus soon attacked other groups as well, and scientists realized that AIDS had been killing heterosexual people in Africa for years before it reached the United

AIDS Across the Globe

In 2003, the estimated number of deaths from AIDS in the United States was 18,017, including 17,934 adults and adolescents and 83 children under age thirteen. The total estimated number of deaths of persons with AIDS in the United States from 1981 to 2003 is 524,060, including 518,568 adults and adolescents and 5,492 children under age thirteen. About a million people in the United States are thought to be infected.

It is estimated that between 35 and 42 million people are living with HIV/AIDS worldwide. The highest estimates for people living with HIV/AIDS are in the following places:

- Sub-Saharan Africa (around 25 million)
- South and Southeast Asia (6.5 million)
- Latin America (around 1.6 million)
- Eastern Europe and Central Asia (around 1.3 million)

Around 4.8 million people were newly infected with HIV/AIDS during 2003. The highest estimates for new HIV/AIDS infections occurring during 2003 are in the following places:

- Sub-Saharan Africa (around 3 million)
- South and Southeast Asia (around 850,000)
- Eastern Europe and Central Asia (around 360,000)
- East Asia and Pacific Islands (around 200,000)

It is estimated that around 3 million people died from HIV/AIDS in 2003. The highest estimates for deaths due to HIV/AIDS during 2003 are in the following places:

- Sub-Saharan Africa (around 2.2 million)
- South and Southeast Asia (around 460,000)
- Latin America (around 84,000)
- East Asia and Pacific Islands (around 44,000)

More than 20 million people have died of AIDS since 1981. By December 2004, women accounted for 47 percent of all people living with HIV worldwide, and for 57 percent in sub-Saharan Africa.

Young people (fifteen to twenty-four years old) account for half of all new HIV infections worldwide—more than 6,000 become infected with HIV every day.

Of the 6.5 million people in developing and transitional countries who need life-saving AIDS drugs, fewer than 1 million are receiving them.

States, but had probably been mistaken for other diseases.

The virus is transmitted by blood as well as sexually, and almost no one is immune. Drug addicts who shared needles became infected. So did transfusion recipients, because the virus had gotten into the blood supply from donors who had no idea they were infected when they gave blood; the incubation period lasts years and people can pass the virus to others long before they get sick. People with the bleeding disorder hemophilia were especially hard hit, because they needed treatments made of blood pooled from many donors. Women are at least as vulnerable as men when it comes to contracting the virus through sex, and mothers can infect their babies at birth or through breast milk.

Where did HIV come from? Researchers believe it originated in west-central Africa, perhaps as early as 1930, when a related virus that normally infects chimpanzees—without making them sick—managed to jump species to a human, probably someone who was cut, scratched, or bitten while hunting the animals or butchering them for food. Chimpanzees, in turn, are thought to have picked up the virus from eating two types of monkeys, red-capped mangabeys and spot-nosed guenons, which carry related viruses and also do not get sick from them.

The earliest known human infection, found recently in a frozen blood sample, occurred in a man who died in 1959. Cases probably occurred repeatedly in Africa over the years but were blamed on other diseases until finally there were so many deaths that they could no longer be overlooked. Why AIDS seemed suddenly to explode into an epidemic in Africa is not clear. The cases may have been building up gradually, or social changes in Africa may have accelerated the spread of the virus, such as a population shift into overcrowded African cities, the growth of prostitution, and the practice of giving injections without sterilizing needles between patients. Exactly how and when the virus came from Africa to North America is not known.

Children wave to a cameraman in Mozambique in 2005. The AIDS epidemic has left more than twelve million African children without parents.

Today, in the United States and other developed countries, AIDS is no longer a death sentence. People do still die from it, but combinations of antiviral drugs have been keeping millions of patients alive for decades. The drugs are no quick fix, though: they can have serious side effects and most patients wish they weren't needed. And the medicines are too expensive for people in much of Africa, so millions there go untreated and die every year.

The ideal strategy, of course, is prevention. Many countries have AIDS education campaigns that urge people to use condoms, limit their number of sexual partners, and avoid needle sharing. But those measures can go only so far. A vaccine is desperately needed. Researchers have been trying for twenty years to create one. So far, they have not succeeded.

Hantavirus Pulmonary Syndrome
First recognized: 1993
Region of origin: Four Corners region, American Southwest
Host animal: Deer mice and other small rodents
Virus family: Bunyaviruses
Number of cases: 396 (1993–2005)
Number of deaths: 143
Outlook for the future: Outbreaks are possible whenever rodent populations explode and rodents invade people's houses.

Death in the Southwest

Suddenly, he could not breathe. A young Navajo man, nineteen years old, was riding in a car with his family near Thoreau, New Mexico, when disaster struck. They veered off the road to a store with a telephone, made a desperate call for help, and he was rushed to the Indian Health Center, thirty miles west in Gallup. Doctors struggled to save him, but could not. They were mystified. Except for a few days of what had seemed like the flu, his family said, there was nothing wrong with him. He was always healthy and athletic; he'd been a cross-country star in high school. How, then, to explain his chest x-ray? His lungs were flooded, so full of fluid that it had cut off his air supply, in effect suffocating him.

Puzzlement turned to alarm when the doctors found out where the young man was going when he collapsed: to his fiancée's funeral. She had died five days earlier, with symptoms exactly like his.

And so it began. One doctor phoned another: Have you seen anything like this? Again and again, the answer was yes: at least five healthy young people in the region had died in the same way recently, from short, unexplained illnesses that swamped their lungs. The Indian Health Service called the state health department; the state called the federal Centers for Disease Control and Prevention.

"MYSTERY FLU KILLS 6 IN TRIBAL AREA," announced the headline of a statewide newspaper on May 17, 1993. Soon a dozen more cases were found around the Four Corners, where the borders of New Mexico, Arizona, Colorado, and Utah meet. Of eighteen victims, ten died.

I was living in Albuquerque, New Mexico, when this terrifying illness broke out. It was hard to fathom. The high desert, with its clear, dry, thin air and brilliant sun seemed like the world's least likely setting for a lung disease; in fact, people used to go there to get over lung ailments like tuberculosis, and some still go hoping the climate will ease their asthma.

Jones Benally, a Navajo "medicine man" hired by the Indian Health Service, stands in front of the ceremonial hogan that serves as his office.

But the outbreak was real. People all over the Southwest were frightened. Tourists canceled trips—but reporters and TV crews descended on the 25,000-square-mile (64,750-square-kilometer) Navajo reservation.

Navajos were angry and distraught. Tradition calls for a private, four-

day mourning period, and during that time the family does not even speak of the deceased. Even after the four days are up, names of the deceased are rarely mentioned. But the outsiders photographed funerals, printed victims' names, and tried to question bereaved families. Local residents began posting NO MEDIA signs on reservation roads, and resentment ran so high that some people refused to cooperate with medical investigators.

A twenty-year-old Navajo man was one of the early victims of the hantavirus outbreak in New Mexico.

Meanwhile, scientists were running tests for every known toxin and every known infection that might have caused such devastating lung damage: poison gas, pesticides, heavy metals, influenza, anthrax, and a host of other bacteria and viruses. They made sure to check for plague, because prairie dogs and their fleas harbor it, and cases still occur from time to time in the Southwest. Every test came up negative. The only logical explanation was that the culprit must be a "new agent."

There was one stroke of luck: whatever the agent was, it did not seem to spread from one person to another, so sick patients did not infect other people, and the number of cases did not explode.

The nature of the disease helped guide the researchers as they investigated further. Its hallmark was the sudden flooding of the lungs. They didn't fill with pus, as in pneumonia, but rather with plasma, the clear, yellowish fluid part of the blood. The plasma leaked into the lungs because the illness somehow produced tiny openings in the walls of capillaries, which are small blood vessels—openings too narrow for blood cells but plenty big enough for plasma. The leaking was like bleeding, but without blood cells.

The capillary leak made researchers think of viruses that cause internal bleeding—hemorrhagic fever viruses like Marburg and Ebola. Another aspect of the disease—high counts of white blood cells—suggested a different group of hemorrhagic viruses, hantaviruses. But doctors knew of no hemorrhagic fevers native to North America, and none of the patients had traveled overseas or been around visitors from Africa, Asia, or South America.

On June 4, scientists at the CDC identified the culprit. It was indeed a new agent—a hantavirus that had never been seen before. The disease it caused became known as hantavirus pulmonary syndrome.

Hantaviruses are a well-known source of sickness in Asia and parts of Europe. They are carried by rodents, and often there is at least one rodent species that can harbor the virus without getting sick from it.

Many scientists were shocked by the finding, because no hantavirus had ever been proved to cause human disease in the United States. And all the known hantaviruses in other parts of the world caused bleeding in the kidneys, not flooding of the lungs.

At the time, Stephen Morse of Rockefeller University, an expert on emerging viruses, said, "We never dreamed of a scenario like this. It would have seemed too close to fiction."

Once researchers knew they were dealing with a hantavirus, they began looking for its carrier by setting hundreds of rodent traps around homes in the Four Corners. Over two months, they dissected some 1,900 rodents

Deer mice sparked the outbreak of hantavirus by carrying it into homes in New Mexico.

THE POWER OF THE MOUSE

Long before the hantavirus outbreak of 1993, Navajo culture strictly prohibited contact with mice. Tradition says that mice brought life to the world by spreading seeds, and so should be revered—but they are also thought to have dangerous powers. They belong to the night world and people belong to the day world, and the two must remain apart. Mice must be kept out of houses and away from food, and should never be touched. If a mouse so much as touches even your clothing, the clothing has to be burned.

"The mouse is the only rodent that Navajos have this thing about," said Dr. Ben Muneta, a physician and CDC-trained epidemiologist who worked for the Indian Health Service at the time of the outbreak. That spring, Dr. Muneta, who is Navajo and speaks the language, went to the Four Corners to find out what native healers might know about the disease.

From a medicine woman Dr. Muneta learned that mice are "bearers of illness from ancient times." Their droppings and saliva are believed to cause disease. Anything a mouse touches might be contaminated, hence the requirement to burn clothing. The Navajo word for mouse, *na'atoosi*, means "the one that sucks on things." The implication, Dr. Muneta said, is that it leaves behind its saliva.

"The illness spreads in the air," he said the medicine woman told him. "In a closed room, the power of the mouse would take over and destroy you if it got in your eyes or nose or mouth."

To Dr. Muneta the scientist, the power of the mouse meant the airborne viral particles that spread the disease.

The medicine woman also told him that "the mouse would choose the strongest and best person in the house." She was right: unlike many other infections, hantaviral diseases are more likely to strike young, healthy people than small children and the elderly.

"It was an incredible feeling of discovery," Dr. Muneta said. "She was describing quite subtle aspects of the infection." He concluded that Navajos must have encountered the hantavirus generations ago and, through astute observation, figured out how to avoid it. "The traditional healers are also scientists, with centuries of experience," he said.

Most families on the reservation knew bits and pieces of the teachings, said Dr. Muneta, who heard some of them himself while growing up. But fewer and fewer people knew the reasons for the old teachings. Young people are especially likely to regard them as embarrassing superstitions.

"Burn your clothes? It doesn't make sense," Dr. Muneta said—unless you know the thinking behind it.

and shipped nearly 10,000 vials of blood and organ samples to the CDC.

Before they had even finished, they had a strong suspect. Again and again, they found the hantavirus in the common deer mouse, *Peromyscus maniculatus*. It was the perfect host, brimming with the virus and not in the least bit sick.

"It's hard to believe such an adorable little animal could cause so much trouble," said Dr. Robert Parmenter, a biologist at the University of New Mexico.

Indeed, *Peromyscus* looks like your basic storybook mouse, with tawny fur, big shiny eyes, long dark whiskers, and an inquisitive snout. Deer mice love getting into people's houses, and they are good at it, capable of squeezing through the tiniest openings. "It's condominiums for them," Dr. Parmenter said.

People can get infected if they touch, inhale, or swallow mouse urine, saliva, or droppings, which are teeming with the virus. As soon as the rodent connection was found, health officials all over the Southwest began urging people to seal their homes against mice, set mousetraps, and use bleach or other disinfectants to clean up any mouse-infested areas.

But deer mice and hantaviruses had probably been around for thousands of years. Why did people suddenly start getting sick in 1993?

Scientists had two possible answers. First, people probably had gotten sick and died from hantavirus lung disease in years past, but their deaths had probably been blamed on pneumonia or unknown respiratory diseases.

Second, the 1993 outbreak probably occurred because deer mice had a population explosion, thanks to wet weather that produced bumper crops of the seeds, nuts, berries, and insects that they eat.

Since 1993, when there were a total of eighteen cases and ten deaths, New Mexico has had a few hantavirus cases nearly every spring and summer. From 1993 through 2005, the overall total was sixty-five cases, and twenty-seven deaths. So far, 1993 is still the worst year by far.

In the same period, there were 396 cases of hantavirus pulmonary syndrome nationwide, and 36 percent of the patients died—a frighteningly high rate. The disease has been reported in thirty states.

Most of the cases seem to occur in relatively young, healthy people, between their teens and their fifties, rather than the very young or the very old. That age pattern has led researchers to suspect that the victims' own immune system—which tends to be at its strongest between the teens and the fifties—may go overboard and mount such a strong response to the virus that it actually causes some of the lung damage seen in the disease.

Although viruses are often named for the place where they were first identified, that did not happen in this case. Scientists did try out several location names—Four Corners virus, Black Mesa virus, Muerto Canyon virus—but local residents objected, not wanting their region to be linked forever to a deadly disease. So finally a wry scientist came up with a name that everybody accepted—the *sin nombre* virus—meaning "the virus without a name."

Friends of mine who still live in the Southwest can't help but worry about the hantavirus when they sweep out their garages, look for stuff in their sheds, or go camping. The storybook mouse has become the villain in a tale that is too strange and awful to be anything but true.

West Nile Disease

First recognized: Uganda, 1937;
United States, 1999
Region of origin: Africa; Middle East
Host animal: Birds, but a specific natural
host is not known; some species die.
Virus family: Flaviviruses
Number of cases (United States, 2005): 2,944
Number of deaths (United States, 2005): 98
Outlook for the future: It is an established
disease throughout most of the United
States, and cases are expected every year
during mosquito season.

A Jet-Set Germ

Maybe it was a mosquito, or perhaps a bird that hitched a ride to New York on an airplane from Africa or the Middle East. Or perhaps an infected human was the culprit. Nobody knows for sure. But one way or another, some living creature brought the West Nile virus to North America.

If it had not been for one especially sharp doctor, there's no telling how long it might have taken for the invader to be discovered. Truth be told, no one knows for sure when the virus first landed here.

But on August 23, 1999, Dr. Deborah Asnis, an infectious disease specialist at a hospital in Queens, a borough of New York City, called the city health department to report that two elderly patients had an unusual, worrisome illness. It looked like some type of encephalitis, a potentially fatal inflammation of the brain.

Within just a few days, as health officials began to investigate, four more cases cropped up. Patients had fevers, headaches, weakness, tremors, confusion, stiff necks, and paralysis, and they sometimes lapsed into coma. By September 10, more than sixty possible cases were being investigated—and three people had died.

The federal Centers for Disease Control and Prevention identified the disease as St. Louis encephalitis, which is caused by a virus carried by a common mosquito, *Culex pipiens*. In response, the city began spraying pesticide over the affected neighborhoods. But the St. Louis virus had never been found in New York City before, so the discovery puzzled many scientists.

Meanwhile, something strange was happening in another part of the city, the Bronx. Birds were dying: crows by the dozen, and captive birds at the Bronx Zoo as well, flamingos, a cormorant, a pheasant, a bald eagle. Autopsies showed brain hemorrhages, a sign of encephalitis. But it wasn't the St. Louis type. This time, the CDC found something even more bizarre: the West Nile virus, a germ from Africa, west Asia, and the Middle East that had never been found in North America.

The disease centers retested samples from people—and admitted that its first diagnosis had been wrong. The human patients also had the West Nile virus.

An American crow. Dozens of dead crows in the Bronx, New York, were an early sign of the appearance of West Nile disease in the United States.

It was an understandable mistake. The two viruses and the illnesses they cause are similar, and transmitted by the same mosquito, so the error may have happened simply because it had not occurred to scientists to look in New York for a virus normally found on the other side of the world.

That first summer in New York, there were sixty-two severe cases and seven deaths. Steadily and relentlessly, the virus began moving westward. By 2002, it had spread clear across the country. The CDC declared West Nile "permanently established in the Western

Hemisphere" and determined from genetic studies that the strain here probably came from the Middle East.

From 1999 to the end of 2004, there were more than 16,000 cases and 660 deaths.

More than 138 bird species have been infected in this country, and more than 43 mosquito species have been found to transmit the virus. Horses can be infected, too, sometimes fatally. Two vaccines have been developed for them.

There is no specific treatment for West Nile disease, and no vaccine for humans, though researchers are trying to develop both.

Fortunately, most of the time the disease is not severe. Only about 1 in 150 people becomes seriously ill with encephalitis or meningitis, an infection of the membranes around the brain and spinal cord. When brain infection occurs, the death rate is about 9 percent, and survivors may suffer lasting or permanent neurological damage. People with weakened immune systems and those over fifty, especially the very old, are most vulnerable. But about 80 percent of all people who are infected don't even know it, because they never get sick or have any symptoms at all. Another 20 percent may run fevers and suffer from headaches, body aches, swollen glands, nausea, and other symptoms, but they recover in days, or sometimes a few weeks.

Mosquito bites are not the only way to catch the disease. It has spread from mother to fetus in the womb, and from mother to baby during breastfeeding. Most of the children appeared unharmed, but the number of cases has been so small that the risk to fetuses and infants is not known for sure.

In 2002, a troubling cluster of cases occurred: four people contracted the West Nile virus from organ transplants. Unbeknownst to the surgeons who performed the transplants, the donor, an accident victim, had probably been infected by blood transfusions given while doctors

DELICATE BUT DEADLY

Mosquitoes, with their spindly legs and fragile wings, are the flimsiest of insects—and the most powerful. Around the world, billions of new mosquitoes are hatched every day, and more than a million people a year die from mosquito bites, killed by diseases that mosquitoes carry. The females feed on blood, and they can carry diseases from one person to the next, as long as the disease-causing germ can make its way to the mosquito's salivary glands so that it is injected into each victim of a bite.

A yellow fever mosquito. They may seem delicate, but mosquitoes have been the cause of numerous epidemics throughout history.

Malaria alone—caused by a one-celled parasite carried by mosquitoes—kills a million people a year and makes at least 300 million sick. Yellow fever kills 30,000, and dengue may kill half a million or more. Both yellow fever and dengue are caused by viruses, and are considered to be emerging or reemerging diseases. Dengue, present in Africa, Asia, and South America, causes tens of millions of cases a year. Travelers have brought it to the United States, and mosquitoes that live here can carry it, so dengue outbreaks are possible. There is no vaccine.

Yellow fever epidemics caused years of delays in the completion of the Panama Canal in the 1890s and early 1900s, and the work could not be finished until mosquitoes were controlled. Today a vaccine is available, and recommended for people who travel to countries where the disease exists.

There are plenty of reasons to avoid mosquito bites in the United States as well. In addition to carrying the West Nile virus, mosquitoes in the United States can carry several other viruses that cause encephalitis in animals and people, including western equine encephalitis, eastern equine encephalitis, St. Louis encephalitis, and LaCrosse encephalitis. There are no vaccines to prevent those diseases in people. Fortunately, none of them has become as common as West Nile virus.

were trying to treat her injuries. All the recipients got sick, and one died.

The cases showed that the virus could be spread by blood and organ transplants. A test was later developed to screen blood, and since then at least three hundred contaminated units have been found and thrown away, according to the CDC.

But so far there is no test that gives results fast enough to tell whether donor organs are infected. Organs have to be transplanted quickly or they will deteriorate; there is not enough time to wait for the results of the current tests. Doctors say that for people who need transplants, the risk of contracting West Nile and dying from it is much smaller than the risk of dying if the transplant is not done.

But transplant patients are especially vulnerable to infectious diseases because in order to keep their bodies from rejecting their new organs, they take medicines that suppress their immune systems. Researchers estimate that if transplant recipients are infected with West Nile, they are about forty times more likely than other people to develop a serious brain infection.

Indeed, in 2005 another cluster of cases occurred when three transplant recipients contracted the disease, two of whom developed encephalitis and were in comas and in critical condition for weeks. The only way to prevent cases like this, doctors say, is to develop better, faster tests to screen organs before they are transplanted.

A horse is inoculated against West Nile virus.

SARS
First recognized: 2003
Region of origin: Southern China
Host animal: Civets, possibly bats
Virus family: Coronaviruses
Number of cases (worldwide): 8,098
Number of deaths (worldwide): 774
Outlook for the future: The 2003 outbreak died out, but the disease could reemerge.

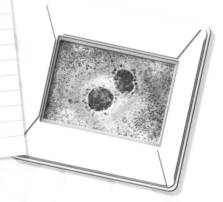

A Delicacy and a Disease

If infectious disease experts have a worst nightmare, it is this: a new, very contagious and severe disease reaches a city that is an international airline hub—a place like Hong Kong, for instance—where infected people then board planes and carry the disease around the world before anyone even notices it.

That is precisely what happened in February and March of 2003, when people in China, Hong Kong, and Vietnam started becoming extremely ill from a disease that came to be called SARS, for severe acute respiratory syndrome.

SARS, like so many other diseases, seemed like the flu at first: it caused a fever, muscle aches, headaches, a dry cough, and a sore throat. But then many patients became short of breath, because the illness infected their lungs, causing pneumonia. As fluid built up in their diseased lungs, some had so much trouble breathing that doctors put them on respirators to pump air directly into their lungs—but they sometimes died anyway. There was no treatment for the disease.

By March 16, there were more than 150 cases and at least 9 deaths, and travelers had also spread the disease to Singapore and Canada. The World Health Organization called SARS a "worldwide health threat." Within a few months, thousands of people were infected in two dozen countries.

Soon, because the epidemic made people afraid to travel to affected areas, it began to hurt business and tourism, ultimately costing the countries billions of dollars. Schools closed in Hong Kong; hotels were empty. In some places hospital employees, afraid of catching the disease, refused to go to work.

Health officials in other countries became angry at China, because the disease apparently started there in late 2002, in the southern province of Guangdong, and yet the Chinese government hid the outbreak from the rest of the world for months. Had China told the truth sooner, many experts say, it might have been possible to prevent SARS from infecting so many people and spreading to other countries.

SARS was amazingly contagious. The disease was spread by coughs and sneezes at close range; people could also catch it by touching a surface a patient had coughed on and then touching their own eyes or mouths. It is also possible, though not known for sure, that SARS germs could stay in the air after a patient coughed or sneezed and infect even people who were not in close contact.

An especially notorious episode began in Hong Kong in February of 2003 at the Hotel Metropole. One guest there, who had caught the disease in southern China, infected about a dozen other hotel guests, some of whom got on airplanes. They carried SARS to more than four hundred people in half a dozen other countries: Vietnam, Singapore, Canada, Germany, the United States, and Ireland. The United States had only eight confirmed cases, all in travelers; none died.

One of the scariest and most fascinating things about SARS was the discovery that some patients seemed to be "superspreaders," capable of

SPREADING SARS

During the 2003 SARS outbreak, an infected traveler from China stayed at the Hotel Metropole in Hong Kong. There, he made contact with other international travelers, who then carried the virus to hospitals around the world. The total count: more than four hundred confirmed infected from one man's visit to the hotel.

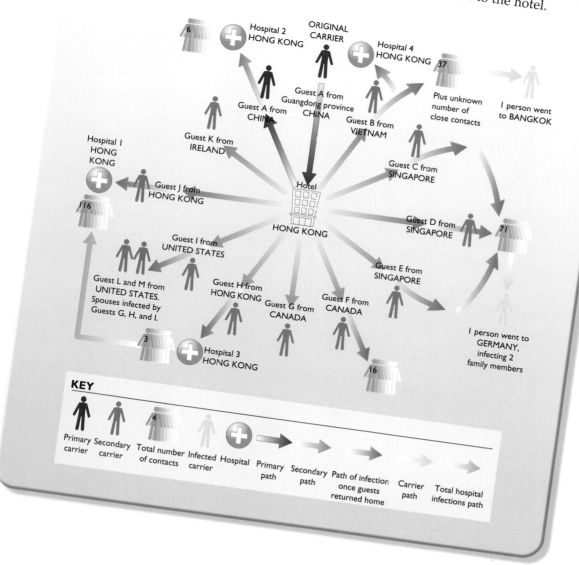

KEY

Primary carrier | Secondary carrier | Total number of contacts | Infected carrier | Hospital | Primary path | Secondary path | Path of infection once guests returned home | Carrier path | Total hospital infections path

infecting huge numbers of other people. In Beijing, for instance, one sixty-two-year-old woman who was sick in the hospital for a week before dying from SARS had close contact with seventy-four other people, including relatives, hospital workers, and other patients—and infected thirty-three of them. They infected others, leading to a total of seventy-six cases that could ultimately be traced back to that first woman. In another case, a seventy-two-year-old man on a flight from Hong Kong to Beijing infected twenty-two other passengers.

It isn't entirely clear why superspreading occurred, but doctors who studied some of the cases found that certain factors seemed to play a role. Older people with severe cases of the disease were more likely than younger, stronger patients to infect others, particularly if the infected person was in the hospital and near other patients who were in a weakened state, vulnerable because they already had another illness. If the disease was not detected quickly and people around the patient therefore were not warned to wear masks and gloves, the odds of infection also went up. In addition, as common sense would suggest, patients who had many close contacts—lots of relatives, visitors, and other people taking care of them—tended to infect more people than did patients who were more isolated.

But what was causing SARS? At first the illness was mistaken for tuberculosis, bacterial pneumonia, or perhaps a severe form of influenza. But lab tests for the germs that usually caused those illnesses came back negative, and the antibiotics that often worked against pneumonia did not help. Doctors began to suspect that they were dealing with a new disease, another emerging infection.

That suspicion proved to be right. Samples of lung tissue, blood, and sputum from patients who died in Asia were sent to the Centers for Disease Control in Atlanta, and what they showed came as a surprise even to scientists.

Young girls en route to a party in Hong Kong wear protective masks as a precaution against the SARS virus in April 2003.

On March 21, 2003, Cynthia Goldsmith, a scientist at the disease centers, used an electron microscope to examine some cells that had been infected by the mystery germ that was causing SARS. The microscope magnified them about 14,000 times.

Telltale features stood out: black beadlike dots of genetic material inside spherical viruses, and viruses lined up along cell surfaces and clustered inside the cells in a certain region called the endoplasmic reticulum.

"My first reaction was 'coronavirus,'" Goldsmith said.

It took her by surprise. Although coronaviruses could make animals very sick, in people they were known to cause only colds and gut trouble, not serious lung diseases. They had not even been mentioned as a culprit in SARS.

But further testing confirmed what Goldsmith saw: SARS was caused by a new type of coronavirus that scientists had never encountered before.

The next piece of the puzzle was where the coronavirus was coming from. One of the first places scientists looked was in the Guangdong province in southern China, where the first cases of SARS had occurred. People there are known to have a taste for all sorts of exotic game, and food markets keep a tremendous variety of wild animals in cages and sell them live for meat—snakes, turtles, badgers, frogs, rats, and other animals are all jammed in cages, waiting for shoppers looking for that night's dinner. Those markets, with different species crowded together and kept in close quarters with people, can be breeding grounds for new diseases. Viruses can jump from one species to another, sometimes changing in the process, and sometimes landing in a new species that gets very, very sick from the invasion.

In May, scientists who tested animals from the markets soon found several species that were infected with the SARS virus: civets, raccoon dogs, and badgers, all considered delicacies in Guangdong. Civets, cat-sized animals that resemble weasels, were more likely to be infected than were the other animals. When the test results came back, China banned sales of the animals.

By the end of July of 2003, at least 8,098 people in twenty-six countries had

A civet peers through the mesh of its cage in an Asian market. Civets were believed to be the source of the virus that caused the SARS epidemic.

contracted SARS, and 774 died. But then the disease died out—thanks largely to old-fashioned disease-control measures, like isolating sick people; making sure that everyone who came near them wore gloves, gowns, and masks; and quarantining people who might have been infected—having them stay home to avoid the risk of spreading the disease until enough time passed to be sure that they were not infected.

When the epidemic subsided, the government allowed civets and the other animals to be sold again for food. Then, in January of 2004, when a man in China came down with SARS, the Chinese government decided that the only way to stamp out the disease was to get rid of civets, and it killed at least 10,000 of them, along with raccoon dogs and badgers. Killing the civets infuriated many people in southern China, who enjoyed civet meat, made their living selling the animals, and did not believe they were a source of disease.

But after the civet slaughter, the only other outbreak, in April of 2004, occurred among laboratory workers who were doing experiments with the virus and accidentally infected themselves.

Even though the epidemic ended, questions remained. It still wasn't clear where SARS really came from. Civets were not widely infected, and those that were got sick and died, which suggested that they were not the natural host of the virus. Scientists kept looking for another host, an animal that could act as a reservoir, harboring the virus without getting sick from it. In September of 2005, two scientific teams reported that they had found an animal—the Chinese horseshoe bat—that seemed to be the hiding place for SARS in nature. Those bats are widely distributed over Asia and parts of Europe.

Now scientists suspect that the SARS coronavirus probably traveled somehow from the bats to the civets in the food markets, and then from civets to people, to cause the epidemic. But they do not know that for sure. And no one can say whether SARS will ever come back.

Monkeypox

First recognized: Monkeys, 1958; humans, 1970 in Africa, 2003 in United States
Region of origin: Africa
Host animal: African squirrels
Virus family: Poxviruses
Number of cases (United States, 2003): 82
Number of deaths: 0 in United States, but 1 to 10 percent death rate in Africa
Outlook for the future: Outbreaks possible if African rodents continue to be imported and sold as pets.

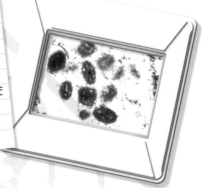

The Pet Connection

Feverish, tired, and aching all over, with swollen glands and pounding heads, the patients seemed at first to have some kind of flu. But May and June aren't exactly the flu season. And people with the flu don't start breaking out in crops of ugly, pus-filled sores that break open, crust, and scab over.

Doctors who saw the first few cases, in Wisconsin in May of 2003, were puzzled and alarmed. Except for the swollen glands, the illness resembled a mild case of smallpox. And initial lab tests detected a virus that belonged to the orthopox family—the group that includes smallpox. Smallpox is one of the world's oldest and most dreaded diseases. Highly contagious, it had a 30 percent death rate historically and killed 300 to 500 million people in the twentieth century alone. Survivors were almost always severely scarred, and some were blinded.

But vaccination wiped out smallpox worldwide by 1980. The virus does not exist in nature. Humans are its only host. The only stocks of the virus now known to exist are locked up in government laboratories in the

United States and Russia. But the disease used to be so widespread that all sorts of people had access to the virus, and there have long been fears that rogue scientists, other countries, or terrorists might have secretly kept samples to use someday as a weapon. After the September 11, 2001, attacks on the World Trade Center and the Pentagon, fears grew tremendously about bioterrorism, especially about smallpox. The government even developed a program to start vaccinating medical workers so that they would be able to take care of victims in the event of a smallpox attack.

Clearly, the only way there could be a smallpox outbreak would be if someone were to start it deliberately. So the sudden appearance of a pox in the Midwest in 2003 was a scary event.

Fortunately, further lab tests at the Centers for Disease Control and Prevention, quickly found that the illness was not smallpox. It was monkeypox.

Monkeypox? That disease, which occurs naturally in rain forests in west and central Africa, had never been found in the United States, or even the Western Hemisphere. It was first discovered in monkeys in Africa in 1958 and named for them, but it also infects many rodents, and African squirrels may be its natural host.

No cases were detected in people until 1970, in Africa. That's when doctors first realized that monkeypox was a zoonosis, an animal disease that can be transmitted to humans.

People can catch monkeypox from animal bites or close contact with an infected animal

In 2003 this family in Dorchester, Wisconsin, caught monkeypox from a pet prairie dog who later died. They decided to keep their other pet prairie dog, pictured here.

SELECT AGENTS AND SPECIAL PATHOGENS

The monkeypox virus, along with dozens of other dangerous germs and poisons, is classified as a "select agent" by the U.S. government. That means it has "the potential to pose a severe threat to public health and safety," and can be handled only by laboratories that have been approved by the Centers for Disease Control and Prevention. Select agents get a lot of attention because, in theory, they could be made into weapons.

Some select agents, like Marburg and Ebola, are also considered "special pathogens." The diseases caused by special pathogens are deadly, and can't be treated or prevented. All are zoonotic, meaning they're carried by animals, and all have to be handled in a special laboratory called a biosafety-level 4 (BSL-4) lab. Researchers in those labs wear sealed space suits that have their own air supplies.

Dr. C. J. Peters, a former head of the CDC's special pathogens branch, described it this way: "The viruses we work with are the ones that can take a perfectly healthy person and kill him in a matter of days."

Only a handful of places in the United States have BSL-4 labs including the CDC, the United States Army Medical Research Institute for Infectious Diseases, and the University of Texas Medical Branch at Galveston.

CDC health officials inspect specimens suspected of being connected to the hantavirus outbreak.

or person. It's a milder disease than smallpox, but it can last for several weeks, and it can be fatal. It has a death rate ranging from 1 to 10 percent, so doctors take it very seriously. There is no cure or specific treatment, but people with severe cases may need to be taken care of in the hospital to get them through the worst stages of the illness.

One of the worst cases in the Midwest outbreak was a ten-year-old girl in Illinois who, covered with sores, was taken to a hospital that had to set up a special isolation unit just for her, to keep the virus from infecting other patients. There is no monkeypox vaccine, but a smallpox vaccination will often prevent monkeypox, so only doctors and nurses who had been vaccinated could take care of her. The sores hurt so much—they even popped up inside her throat—that she sometimes needed morphine. But she survived.

How had an African virus made its way to America? One clue was that all the sick people had had contact with prairie dogs, which had become a fad with pet owners, who sometimes paid as much as $150 apiece for them. The ten-year-old girl had three of them. The prairie dogs turned out to have monkeypox. But prairie dogs are native to the United States. So how did they catch an African virus? Local health officials and epidemiologists from the CDC asked the animals' owners where they had bought their pets.

The trail led to a store called Phil's Pocket Pets, outside Chicago. There, prairie dogs had been kept in close quarters with another trendy, cute, furry pet—a three-pound giant Gambian pouched rat—imported from Ghana, in Africa. The rat was infected, and so were other African rodents like rope squirrels, brush-tailed porcupines, and dormice that had been part of the same shipment of exotic pets from Ghana in April. Phil's had bought them from a dealer in Texas. The shipment contained about eight hundred animals, and the government began trying to trace them all, to have them destroyed, along with all the prairie dogs that might have been exposed to them. That led to an outcry from an organization set up to protect prairie dogs, which said that the animals should be quarantined and watched, and allowed to live if they turned out to not be infected. Nonetheless, health officials ordered the animals killed.

Health departments also appealed to the public, asking people who had bought the pets not to just let them go, because if they were released they could spread the virus to wild animals and monkeypox might become an established disease in the United States.

By June 9, there were twenty-three people with monkeypox symptoms, in Wisconsin, Illinois, and Indiana. A week later, the number of confirmed and suspected cases had jumped to eighty-two, still mostly in the Midwest. One victim was an eleven-year-old boy in New Jersey who diagnosed his own illness after seeing a report about monkeypox on the TV news. His family had recently moved from Indiana, where he had been bitten by two pet prairie dogs at a friend's house.

In Wisconsin, one prairie dog—called a "supertransmitter" by amazed epidemiologists—managed somehow to infect eighteen people in its travels from a pet store to a cage in someone's home, and then to two veterinary clinics.

No one died from the American monkeypox outbreak. But the government banned the importation of African rodents and the sale of prairie dogs as pets. Infectious disease experts had long been warning that sooner or later people were going to get into trouble from their desire to make pets out of wild animals like prairie dogs and adorable creatures from other parts of the world. Long before monkeypox came along, health experts were warning that prairie dogs could be dangerous because they and their fleas can carry bubonic plague.

The international trade in "exotic pets"—parrots, turtles, iguanas, snakes, all sorts of rodents—has done two things that are practically a recipe for spreading exotic diseases and helping them emerge into human populations. First, the trade has transported animals like giant Gambian rats across oceans and brought them together with species that they would never encounter naturally, like prairie dogs. Not much is known about the germs these animals might spread to one another, or what the germs might do inside a new host in a new environment. Second, the trade has brought people close to animals—and to diseases—they had little or no contact with before.

Dr. Frank Fenner, an expert on pox viruses at Australian National University in Canberra, said, "Quite a lot of new viruses have been turning up, all coming out of animal hosts."

And, he cautioned, "I think we know so little about the viruses of wild animals."

Gambian pouched rats carried monkeypox from Africa and spread the virus to other animals that were sold by an exotic pet distributor.

Epilogue

T he viral outbreaks described in this book may seem like weird, isolated events, the likes of which are unlikely to be seen again. But that is not the case.

"Infectious diseases are undergoing a global resurgence and threaten the health of everyone," said a report published in 2000 by the Institute of Medicine, an independent group that advises the government. The report, written by a Nobel prize-winning scientist, Dr. Joshua Lederberg, went on to say that infectious diseases were "the world's greatest killer of children and young adults, accounting for more than 13 million deaths a year and half of all deaths in developing countries." Viral diseases are among the top killers, including influenza, measles, and AIDS. Emerging viruses also play a role in deaths from pneumonia and diarrheal disease.

Diseases that were once well controlled can bounce back, even in developed countries. England had tens of thousands of cases of mumps in 2005, and the United States had more than a thousand in 2006.

Viruses continue to emerge. For instance, the Toscana virus, spread by sandflies and first identified in Italy in 1971, has since become a major cause of nervous system infections—encephalitis and meningitis—in Italy and other Mediterranean countries. In a recent report, a team of doctors from France, Spain, Italy, and Greece wrote that the virus "must be considered an emerging pathogen." But, the researchers say, Toscana is "unstudied," and few doctors are aware of its potential to make people sick. And they warn that if infected people donate blood, the disease could get into the blood supply and be spread by transfusions to patients who are already sick and who may be unable to fight off the virus.

In 2005, three people who received organ transplants in New England died from LCMV, lymphocytic choriomeningitis virus, which is spread by house mice, hamsters, gerbils, and guinea pigs. Three other transplant patients had died the same way in Wisconsin in 2003. Apparently, in both regions the organ donors had been infected, but no one knew it. A hamster owned by the New England donor tested positive for the virus. But the donors themselves did not test positive, probably because they

Members of the WHO meet at their headquarters in Geneva during a 2005 conference on avian flu.

had such low levels of the virus in their blood that tests were not sensitive enough to find it. If this had ever happened before, the cases had not been discovered.

The virus doesn't do much to healthy people: it may cause a mild flulike illness, or cause no symptoms at all (though it can harm the fetus in pregnant women). The infection had gone completely unnoticed in the organ donors. But transplant recipients can become critically ill from the virus. In addition to taking drugs that suppress the immune system, they may also be exposed to a relatively large amount of virus clinging to their new organs. People with weakened immune systems—those with HIV or AIDS, or people receiving some types of chemotherapy for cancer, for instance—may also be very susceptible to this infection, as well as others that do not harm healthy people.

After the deaths of the transplant recipients with LCMV, scientists from the Centers for Disease Control and Prevention tracked two infected hamsters and a guinea pig to a pet seller in Ohio, MidSouth Distributors. Infected animals had to be killed. But the problem has not been wiped out, and the disease centers warn that rodents from any store can still spread a variety of viral diseases.

What can we, as individuals and as nations, do to protect ourselves from emerging viruses? The truth is, we can't always avoid them. We have to live our lives. We can't retreat into germproof bubbles or wash our hands a hundred times a day. People who need transplants have no choice. They are desperately ill, and a donated organ may be their only chance at life. Few would turn it down for fear that it might harbor some unheard-of disease. On the other hand, people with transplants, and others with suppressed immune systems, might think twice about certain types of pets once they learn about the potential risks. The rest of us should probably think twice about buying exotic pets from foreign countries.

SPREADING DISEASE

New diseases will continue to emerge, and old ones to reemerge, as long as certain conditions exist that foster their development. The Institute of Medicine and other health organizations list these factors (and many others) as contributing significantly to emerging disease:

⚠ Increased human intrusion into tropical forests
⚠ Lack of access to health care
⚠ Population growth and changes in demographics
⚠ Inadequate and deteriorating public health systems
⚠ Urbanization and crowding
⚠ Modern travel
⚠ Increased trade and expanded markets for imported foods
⚠ Changing weather patterns
⚠ Failure to use available vaccines
⚠ World trade in exotic pets

Deforestation forces wildlife to find new places to live, often bringing animals, and their diseases, in contact with humans.

Though some outbreaks may be inevitable, it may be possible to nip them in the bud before they turn into raging epidemics. But that means doctors, governments, health officials, and the rest of us need to be aware—not panicky, just mindful—that new infectious diseases can crop up and old ones can come back, especially if vaccinations are stopped before a disease is truly wiped out.

Unusual illnesses and patterns of disease—in people or animals—must be investigated. When healthy people suddenly start dying from a mysterious type of pneumonia or encephalitis, it's important to find out what is causing the illness as quickly as possible. If patients who receive kidney transplants become ill unexpectedly, the donor must be checked. A hemorrhage in a baby should be a cause for alarm, even in an African hospital with lots of sick babies. If the answer can't be found right away, at the very least blood or tissue samples should be saved and frozen for later study.

Extreme weather can cause habitat destruction, as well as breakdowns in sanitation, which often lead to disease.

The World Health Organization tracks disease outbreaks, but it depends on individual countries to monitor themselves—to perform "surveillance" for infectious disease—and report what's happening within their borders. WHO guidelines say that communicating openly about disease outbreaks is as important as having the technical skills to combat the illness.

But countries that find themselves in the grip of an epidemic sometimes deny it and try to hide it for fear of losing tourism and trade. In 2005, for instance, other governments became skeptical about whether China was telling the truth about how many human cases of bird flu were occurring there, because China's figures seemed too low compared to the numbers reported by other Asian countries that had similar conditions and lots of infected birds. The distrust was based partly on the fact that in the past, China did hide the truth about SARS.

When governments try to cover up an epidemic instead of asking for help to stamp it out, the disease keeps spreading, and the longer it goes unchecked, the harder it will be to control. Sooner or later the rest of the world will find out what's going on anyway. The secrecy winds up accomplishing little—but the lost time may cost lives.

In 2006, Angola suffered another deadly epidemic, this time from a bacterial disease, cholera, which made tens of thousands of people sick and killed at least a thousand. Aid groups complained that the government seemed reluctant to help fight the outbreak, or even admit that it existed.

The events described in this book are just chapters in the unfolding story of emerging viruses, a story that shows no signs of ending. How doctors, governments, and individuals react to the lessons that we've learned so far in this story will determine how it unfolds in the future.

SOURCE NOTES

One of my favorite things about being a reporter is that I get to call or visit all sorts of interesting people—doctors, scientists, health officials, citizens nearby or in far-off places—and ask them questions. Everybody has a story, and one source almost always leads to another.

Much of the information in this book came from interviews I conducted while writing news stories for *The New York Times*. But reporters use other resources too, probably some of the same ones as students who are working on projects. We get ideas from other journalists' reporting in newspapers and on the radio and TV. I google things like disease names and look for the names of scientists who have studied them and published research on them. I try to interview those scientists—in person, or on the phone, or sometimes even by e-mail—and often ask them to recommend other experts.

I am very cautious about using information from the Internet, because too often I have found material that is outdated or just plain wrong. I double-check what I find even from sites that I trust, usually by consulting other sources. Anybody can make a mistake.

I regularly scan the contents and often read articles in medical and scientific journals like the *New England Journal of Medicine*, the *Journal of the American Medical Association*, the *Lancet, Science, Nature, Annals of Internal Medicine*, the *Journal of Emerging Infectious Diseases*, and the *Morbidity and Mortality Weekly Report* put out by the U.S. government's Centers for Disease Control and Prevention.

If I want to check on disease outbreaks, I use the Web sites of the CDC, the World Health Organization, and the International Society for Infectious Diseases. (Further information on these Web sites can be found in the "Internet Resources" section of this book.)

For basic information about diseases I sometimes consult the Web site of the National Institutes of Health or the print or online version of the home edition of *The Merck Manual of Medical Information*.

Most important, good reporters try to keep their eyes and ears and minds open all the time. We're always looking for a story.

FURTHER READING

If you want to dig more deeply into the subjects covered in this book, I would suggest two books that were written for adults, *The Hot Zone*, by Richard Preston, and *Virus Hunter*, by C. J. Peters.

You may also enjoy reading the following articles from *The New York Times* (listed here in chronological order by subject):

Animals and Disease

Taubes, Gary. "A Mosquito Bites Back." *The New York Times*, August 24, 1997.

Licata, Paula Ganzi. "Rodents Just Want a Nice Home: Yours." *The New York Times*, October 8, 2000.

Blakeslee, Sandra. "Mad Cows, Sane Cats: Making Sense of the Species Barrier." *The New York Times*, June 3, 2003.

Grady, Denise, and Lawrence K. Altman. "Beyond Cute: Exotic Pets Come Bearing Exotic Germs." *The New York Times*, June 17, 2003.

Lodge, David M. "Biological Hazards Ahead." *The New York Times*, June 19, 2003.

Derr, Mark. "Cute but Wild: The Perilous Lure of Exotic Pets." *The New York Times*, June 24, 2003.

Altman, Lawrence K. "Tackling the Animal-to-Human Link in Illness." *The New York Times*, March 25, 2006.

Avian Flu

Altman, Lawrence K. "Hunt in Sealed Lab Seeks Deadly Secrets of 'Bird Flu.'" *The New York Times*, January 13, 1998.

Kolata, Gina. "Gain in Hunt for How a Flu Virus Turns Lethal." *The New York Times*, September 7, 2001.

Bradsher, Keith, and Lawrence K. Altman. "A War and a Mystery; Confronting Avian Flu." *The New York Times*, October 12, 2004.

Reynolds, Gretchen. "The Flu Hunters." *The New York Times*, November 7, 2004.

Kolata, Gina. "Experts Unlock Clues to Spread of 1918 Flu Virus." *The New York Times*, October 6, 2005.

Grady, Denise. "Danger of Flu Pandemic Is Clear, if Not Present." *The New York Times*, October 9, 2005.

Pollack, Andrew. "Lessons from a Plague That Wasn't." *The New York Times*, October 23, 2005.

Shreeve, Jamie. "Why Revive a Deadly Flu Virus?" *The New York Times*, January 29, 2006.

Grady, Denise. "Making a Ferret Sneeze for Hints to the Transmission of Bird Flu." *The New York Times*, March 27, 2006.

Grady, Denise, and Gina Kolata. "Q & A: How Serious Is the risk of Avian Flu?" *The New York Times*, March 27, 2006.

McNeil, Donald G., Jr. "The Worrier: At the U.N.: This Virus Has an Expert 'Quite Scared.'" *The New York Times*, March 27, 2006.

Rosenthal, Elizabeth. "The Skeptic: On the Front: A Pandemic Is Worrisome but 'Unlikely.'" *The New York Times*, March 27, 2006.

Bioterrorism

Rosenthal, Elisabeth. "Turning a Flu Virus into a Weapon." *The New York Times*, August 28, 2002.

Altman, Lawrence K. "Disease Control Center Bolsters Terror Response." *The New York Times*, August 28, 2002.

Stolberg, Sheryl Gay, and Judith Miller. "Threats and Responses: Bioterrorism." *The New York Times*, September 9, 2002.

Emerging Diseases

Altman, Lawrence K. "Infectious Diseases on the Rebound in the U.S., a Report Says." *The New York Times*, May 10, 1994.

Wade, Nicholas. "Method and Madness: The Next Plague, and the Next." *The New York Times*, September 25, 1994.

Altman, Lawrence K. "What Is the Next Plague?" *The New York Times*, November 11, 2003.

Altman, Lawrence K. "New Microbes Could Become the 'New Norm.'" *The New York Times*, March 9, 2004.

Epidemiology

Wadler, Joyce. "Passionate Life in a Lab with Dead Animals." *The New York Times*, October 1, 1999.

Zuger, Abigail. "Scientist at Work: C. J. Peters: A Baffling Viral Outbreak? He's on the Trail." *The New York Times*, August 14, 2001.

Altman, Lawrence K. "The Doctor's World: A Specialist in Fighting New Diseases Is Chosen to Wipe Out an Old One." *The New York Times*, August 12, 2003.

Altman, Lawrence K. "The Doctor's World: Her Job: Helping Save the World from Bird Flu." *The New York Times*, August 9, 2005.

Global Warming and Disease

Stevens, William K. "Warmer, Wetter, Sicker: Linking Climate to Health." *The New York Times*, August 10, 1998.

Globalization and Disease

Revkin, Andrew C. "Mosquito Virus Exposes a Hole in the Safety Net." *The New York Times*, October 4, 1999.

Goldberg, Jeffrey. "Microbes on the Move." *The New York Times*, October 10, 1999.

Ho, Andy. "Why Epidemics Still Surprise Us." *The New York Times*, April 1, 2003.

Hantavirus
Brooke, James. "Lethal Virus Borne by Mice Makes Return in the West." *The New York Times*, June 25, 1998.

Nagourney, Eric. "Hantavirus Found Near the Beaten Track." *The New York Times*, February 27, 2001.

Glaberson, William. "Death of a Young Navajo Casts the Spotlight on a Rare Virus." *The New York Times*, April 23, 2001.

Ray, C. Claiborne. "Q & A: Mice and Hantavirus." *The New York Times*, April 20, 2004.

HIV/AIDS
Henig, Robin Marantz. "AIDS: A New Disease's Deadly Odyssey." *The New York Times*, February 6, 1983.

"The Source of AIDS." *The New York Times*, February 2, 1999.

Altman, Lawrence K. "AIDS Virus Originated Around 1930, Study Says." *The New York Times*, February 2, 2000.

"The Global Plague of AIDS." *The New York Times*, April 23, 2000.

Kolata, Gina. "When H.I.V. Made Its Jump to People" *The New York Times*, January 29, 2002.

Gates, Bill. "Slowing the Spread of AIDS in India." *The New York Times*, November 9, 2002.

Dugger, Celia W. "Devastated by AIDS, Africa Sees Life Expectancy Plunge." *The New York Times*, July 16, 2004.

Wines, Michael, and Sharon LaFraniere. "Hut by Hut, AIDS Steals Life in a Southern Africa Town." *The New York Times*, November 28, 2004.

Altman, Lawrence K. "A U.N. Report Takes a Hard Look at Fighting AIDS in Africa." *The New York Times*, March 5, 2005.

Pogash, Carol. "The Inexplicable Survivors of a Widespread Epidemic." *The New York Times*, May 3, 2005.

Altman, Lawrence K. "Gains Made to Contain AIDS but Its Global Spread Goes on, U.N. Says." *The New York Times*, June 3, 2005.

Marburg Fever
"Green Monkey Fever." *The New York Times*, November 3, 1976.

Fisher, Ian. "63 Deaths in Congo Laid to Virus Akin to Ebola." *The New York Times*, May 7, 1999.

Wines, Michael. "Virus New to Angola Kills 95; Travelers Told to Avoid North." *The New York Times*, March 24, 2005.

LaFraniere, Sharon, and Denise Grady. "Fear and Violence Accompany a Deadly Virus Across Angola." *The New York Times*, April 9, 2005.

LaFraniere, Sharon. "To Contain Virus in Angola, Group Wants Hospital Closed." *The New York Times*, April 10, 2005.

LaFraniere, Sharon. "Health Workers Battle Virus in Angola." *The New York Times*, April 11, 2005.

LaFraniere, Sharon, and Denise Grady. "A Daunting Search: Tracking a Deadly Virus in Angola." *The New York Times*, April 12, 2005.

Grady, Denise. "In Angola's Teeming Capital, a Suspected Virus Carrier Dies Alone." *The New York Times*, April 12, 2005.

LaFraniere, Sharon, and Denise Grady. "Stalking a Deadly Virus, Battling a Town's Fears." *The New York Times*, April 17, 2005.

Grady, Denise. "Deadly Virus Alters Angola's Traditions." *The New York Times*, April 19, 2005.

LaFraniere, Sharon. "Specialists Say 'Healers' in Angola Are Helping to Spread Deadly Virus." *The New York Times*, April 25, 2005.

Grady, Denise. "Mysterious Viruses as Bad as They Get." *The New York Times*, April 26, 2005.

Grady, Denise. "Hospital Errors Jeopardize Angola Virus Battle." *The New York Times*, April 30, 2005.

Grady, Denise. "Marburg Virus Toll at 311." *The New York Times*, May 20, 2005.

Grady, Denise. "Marburg Cases Baffle Authorities in Angola." *The New York Times*, May 24, 2005.

Grady, Denise. "New Vaccines Prevent Ebola and Marburg in Monkeys." *The New York Times*, June 6, 2005.

"End of Deadly Epidemic Declared." *The New York Times*, November 9, 2005.

Monkeypox in the United States
Altman, Lawrence K. "Less Lethal Cousin of Smallpox Arrives in the U.S." *The New York Times*, June 9, 2003.

Wilgoren, Jodi. "Monkeypox Casts Light on Rule Gap for Exotic Pets." *The New York Times*, June 10, 2003.

Davey, Monica, with Lawrence K. Altman. "Suspected Cases of Monkeypox Are Rising." *The New York Times*, June 10, 2003.

"The Monkeypox Warning." *The New York Times*, June 11, 2003.

"Suspected Case of Monkeypox Is Investigated in New Jersey." *The New York Times*, June 11, 2003.

Altman, Lawrence K. "As Monkeypox Rises, Smallpox Vaccines Will Be Offered." *The New York Times*, June 11, 2003.

Altman, Lawrence K. "Smallpox Vaccinations Are Urged and Prairie Dogs Are Banned to Halt Monkeypox." *The New York Times*, June 12, 2003.

Altman, Lawrence K. "Patient May Have Transmitted Monkeypox." *The New York Times,* June 13, 2003.

Altman, Lawrence K. "One Prairie Dog Played Critical Role in Wisconsin." *The New York Times,* June 14, 2003.

Altman, Lawrence K. "U.S. Health Official Is Optimistic on Containing Monkeypox Virus." *The New York Times,* June 20, 2003.

McNeil, Donald G., Jr. "Death Sought for Animals in Monkeypox Case." *The New York Times,* July 3, 2003.

Healy, Patrick. "Prairie Dogs Are Euthanized Amid Fears of Monkeypox." *The New York Times,* July 6, 2003.

SARS
Altman, Lawrence K., and Keith Bradsher. "Rare Health Alert Is Issued by W.H.O. for Mystery Illness." *The New York Times,* March 16, 2003.

Altman, Lawrence K., and Elizabeth Rosenthal. "Health Organization Stepping Up Efforts to Find Cause of Mysterious Illness." *The New York Times,* March 18, 2003.

Bradsher, Keith. "A Deadly Virus on Its Mind, Hong Kong Covers Its Face." *The New York Times,* March 31, 2003.

"Responses to Growing Outbreak." *The New York Times,* April 2, 2003.

Bradsher, Keith. "From Tourism to High Finance, Mysterious Illness Spreads Havoc." *The New York Times,* April 3, 2003.

Grady, Denise. "Fear Reigns as Dangerous Mystery Illness Spreads." *The New York Times,* April 7, 2003.

McNeil, Donald G., Jr., "Health Officials Wield a Big Stick, Carefully, Against SARS." *The New York Times,* April 20, 2003.

Eckholm, Erik. "Illness's Psychological Impact in China Exceeds Its Actual Numbers." *The New York Times,* April 24, 2003.

Bradsher, Keith. 'Hong Kong Doctor's Ordeal as Patient with New Disease." *The New York Times,* April 26, 2003.

Grady, Denise. "Health Group Relies on a Time-Tested Rule to Determine Last New Case." *The New York Times,* April 29, 2003.

"The Cost of SARS." *The New York Times,* May 1, 2003.

Altman, Lawrence K., and Denise Grady. "Study Says Virus Has Remained Stable, Not Weakening as the Illness Spreads." *The New York Times,* May 9, 2003.

Bradsher, Keith. "SARS Declared Contained, with No Cases in Past 20 Days." *The New York Times,* July 6, 2003.

Superspreaders
McNeil, Donald G., Jr., and Lawrence Altman. "How One Person Can Fuel an Epidemic." *The New York Times,* April 15, 2003.

Kahn, Joseph. "'Superspreader': Man's Virus Infects Town, Killing His Family." *The New York Times,* May 15, 2003.

West Nile Disease in the U.S.
Steinhauer, Jennifer. "African Virus May Be the Culprit in Mosquito-Borne Illness." *The New York Times,* September 25, 1999.

Revkin, Andrew C. "Latest Battle with Virus to Be Fought in Backyards.' *The New York Times,* March 24, 2000.

Chen, David W. "Lives That Have Been Changed Forever from the Aftereffects of a Mosquito Bite." *The New York Times,* August 19, 2000.

Woodside, Christine. "Sorting Out the Danger of the West Nile Virus." *The New York Times,* September 10, 2000.

Kennedy, Randy. "Man Versus Mosquito." *The New York Times,* September 17, 2000.

Kilborn, Peter T. "All 50 States Now Warn of West Nile Virus Threat." *The New York Times,* August 16, 2002.

AP. "New Test Finds West Nile in Donated Blood." *The New York Times,* July 4, 2003.

Pérez-Peña, Richard. "Donor's Organs Are Linked to West Nile." *The New York Times,* October 7, 2005.

INTERNET RESOURCES

There are dozens of sites on the World Wide Web that provide updated information on emerging diseases and global health. The following are good sources for further research:

The International Society for Infectious Diseases: www.promedmail.org

The World Health Organization: www.who.int

The Centers for Disease Control and Prevention: www.cdc.gov

National Center for Infectious Diseases: www.cdc.gov/ncidod/

The Infectious Disease Society of America: www.idsociety.org

Center for Infectious Disease Research & Policy, University of Minnesota: www.cidrap.umn.edu

The journal *Emerging Infectious Diseases*, published by the Centers for Disease Control and Prevention: www.cdc.gov/ncidod/EID

The National Institute of Allergy and Infectious Diseases: www3.niaid.nih.gov

For information about Angola from the U.S. government, see www.cia.gov/cia/publications/factbook/geos/ao.html and travel.state.gov/travel/cis_pa_tw/cis/cis_1096.html.

To learn more about the humanitarian group Doctors Without Borders, visit www.doctorswithoutborders.org.

For information about government research in infectious disease and bioterrorism, visit the U.S. Army Medical Research Institute of Infectious Diseases site at www.usamriid.army.mil.

ACKNOWLEDGMENTS

Many people were generous with their time and talent, and I could not have written this book without their help. Alex Ward of *The New York Times* and Deirdre Langeland of Kingfisher Publications provided invaluable ideas, advice, encouragement, and thoughtful editing. Maggie Berkvist brought creativity and skill to the search for images that would bring the text to life. My husband, Robert Saar, cheerfully endured a lot of late nights and shut-in weekends. Laura Chang, science editor at *The Times,* kindly agreed to share my time and attention with this project. She and the other editors of the science department and the foreign desk understood what was happening in Angola and mobilized quickly to help get me there. Sharon LaFraniere, a talented reporter and writer, paved the way in Uige and was an extraordinary and inspiring colleague. Evelyn Hockstein's haunting and evocative photographs made our stories real. It would have been impossible to report on the medical efforts in Uige without Dave Daigle, a tireless press officer for the Centers for Disease Control and Prevention, who always managed to balance reporters' requests with the needs of the medical teams who were struggling to control the Marburg outbreak. Dick Thompson of the World Health Organization also helped me make vital connections. Most important of all, the citizens of Uige were gracious hosts who shared their stories and some of the most painful moments of their lives during a time of great fear and suffering.

Picture Credits

The publisher would like to thank the following for permission to reproduce their material. Every care has been taken to trace copyright holders. However, if there have been unintentional omissions, we apologize and will, if informed, endeavor to make corrections in any future edition.

Cover: Centers for Disease Control and Prevention/Science Photo Library, London. Pages 2–3 (left to right): Alexander Joe/AFP/Getty Images, Abid Katib/Getty Images, Evelyn Hockstein/Polaris, Christian Keenan/Getty Images, Martin Harvey/Corbis, Evelyn Hockstein/ Polaris, Evelyn Hockstein/Polaris; 6–7 (left to right): Science Source/Photo Researchers, Visuals Unlimited/Corbis, BSIP, James Cavallini/Science Photo Library, Chris Bjornberg/Photo Researchers, Scott Camarzine/Photo Researchers, CAMR/A.B. Dowsett/Photo Researchers, Kingfisher Photo Archives; 8: Science Source/Photo Researchers; 11: Al Fenn/Time Life Pictures/Getty Images; 13: Jochen Tack/Alamy; 15: Reuters/Corbis; 18–19: Mike Hutchings/Reuters/Corbis; 21: Evelyn Hockstein/Polaris; 23: Alexander Joe/AFP/Getty Images; 24: Alexander Joe/AFP/Getty Images; 28: Christopher Black/WHO; 31: Evelyn Hockstein/Polaris; 34–35: Evelyn Hockstein/Polaris (all); 36: Florence Panoussian/AFP/Getty Images; 41: Florence Panoussian/AFP/Getty Images; 45: Doctors with Africa CUAMM/AP; 47: Doctors with Africa CUAMM/AP; 50: Reuters/Corbis; 55: Evelyn Hockstein/Polaris; 57: Evelyn Hockstein/Polaris; 61: LUSA/Francisco Ribeiro/AP; 62: Abid Katib/Getty Images; 66: Jacob Silberberg/AP; 68: Martin Harvey/Corbis (left), Mike Lane /Woodfall.com; 70: Visuals Unlimited/Corbis; 72: Science Source/Photo Researchers; 73: David N. Davis/Photo Researchers; 74: Ken Bereskin; 75: Florence Panoussin/AFP/Getty Images; 76: Visuals Unlimited/Corbis; 78: Adrian Bradshaw/EPA; 81: BSIP, James Cavallini/Science Photo Library; 82: Jeffrey Markowitz/Corbis; 86: Graeme Robertson/Getty Images; 87: Chris Bjornberg/Photo Researchers; 88: Marc F. Henning/Daily Times/AP; 89: Barbara Laing/Time Life Pictures/Getty Images; 90: James Gathany/CDC; 94: Scott Camazine/Photo Researchers; 95: Gilbert S. Grant/Photo Researchers; 97: Jim Gathany/CDC; 98: Ed Andrieski/AP; 99: CAMR/A.B.Dowsett/Photo Researchers; 103: Christian Keenan/Getty images; 104: Paul Hilton/EPA; 107: Mike Roemer/Getty Images; 108: CDC/Corbis; 111: Courtesy Lincoln Park Zoo, Chicago; 113: Fabrice Coffrini/AFP/Getty Images; 115: Martin Harvey/Corbis; 116: Mike Theiss/Jim Reed Photograph/Corbis.

INDEX

Bold page numbers
refer to maps
or photos.

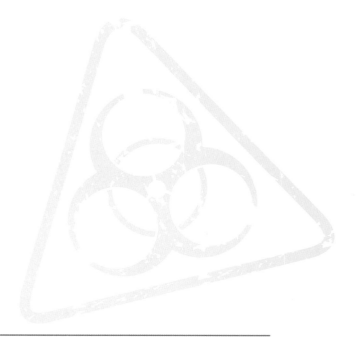

Green Monkey Fever November 3, 1976 • Nairobi Aides Suspect Outbreak of Green Monkey Viral Disease Februa
Toll Grows April 2, 2005 • Angola: Marburg Virus Claims More Lives April 5, 2005 • Fear and Violence Accomp
2005 • A Daunting Search: Tracking a Deadly Virus in Angola April 12, 2005 • In Angola's Teeming Capital, a
• Specialists Say "Healers" in Angola Are Helping to Spread Deadly Virus April 25, 2005 • Marburg Virus To
Declared November 9, 2005 • Rare Health Alert Is Issued by W.H.O. for Mystery Illness March 16, 2003 • Chin
Cause of Mysterious Illness March 18, 2003 • Researchers Find Clues That a Virus Is Causing the Mysterious
Crude Test Offers Hope for Tracking Mystery Virus March 22, 2003 • Fear of New Virus Grows as Hong Kong Off
Mystery Virus Leads to Hong Kong Quarantine April 1, 2003 • Hong Kong: Virus Imperils Commerce and Econ
Beijing's Total of Infected Is Revised Up, to Over 50 April 5, 2003 • Hong Kong Hospitals Struggle as Disease
Say Disease May Be Here to Stay April 9, 2003 • Virus Called Mostly Under Control April 12, 2003 • Youth and
• Death Rate From SARS More Than Doubles, Varying Sharply by Country April 22, 2003 • Travelers Urged to
28, 2003 • Health Group Relies on a Time-Tested Rule to Determine Last New Case April 29, 2003 • SARS Is
"Superspreader": Man's Virus Infects Town, Killing His Family May 15, 2003 • Relieved Hong Kong Starts to S
Regions June 14, 2003 • Hong Kong Off SARS List June 24, 2003 • Canada: SARS All-Clear July 3, 2003 • SARS
June 11, 1993 • Rodent-Virus Death Toll Rises June 25, 1993 • Health Officials Fear Spread of a Deadly Virus
Southern California Mice September 19, 1993 • Virus That Caused Deaths Among Navajos Is Isolated November 21
Illness to Tribe April 24, 1994 • Hantavirus Claims a Miner in Nevada November 26, 1995 • Cases of Fatal Viru
Rodent Virus Strikes People in Patagonia December 8, 1996 • Virus Kills 13 in Chile, Alarming Other Countrie
Threat from Infected Mice February 16, 1999 • Rare Virus Afflicts Girl May 23, 2000 • Death of a
Mosquito-Borne Illness September 25, 1999 • Exotic Virus Is Identified in 3 Deaths September 26, 1999 • Fifth
1999 • West Nile Virus Found in Bird in Maryland October 30, 1999 • Plan to Fight West Nile Virus Outlined
Virus Cause Concern March 16, 2000 • '99 West Nile Virus Infected up to 1,900 People in Queens March 24, 200
Seems Settled In August 8, 2000 • Lives That Have Been Changed Forever from the Aftereffects of a Mosquito B
Finding of West Nile Virus August 3, 2001 • Four Are Killed in Outbreak of West Nile Virus on Gulf Coast Au
Nile Virus Threat June 22, 2003 • Alabama: West Nile Kills Woman June 29, 2003 • New Test Finds West Nile i
Bring West Nile Virus to Colorado August 18, 2003 • Wyoming Checks Mine for West Nile Source October 28, 2003
October 7, 2005 • Less Lethal Cousin of Smallpox Arrives in the U.S. June 9, 2003 • Prairie Dogs Are Blamed
Rising June 10, 2003 • Smallpox Vaccinations Are Urged and Prairie Dogs Are Banned to Halt Monkeypox June
Monkeypox Virus June 20, 2003 • Prairie Dogs Are Euthanized Amid Fears of Monkeypox July 6, 2003 • Pou
Reaches Michigan August 16, 1987 • Global Flu Risk Seen in Asia Fish Farms January 28, 1988 • Avian Flu St
Avian Flu Transmitted to Doctor, Officials Say December 27, 1997 • Hong Kong to Inspect Mainland Farms for
Gain in Hunt for How a Flu Virus Turns Lethal September 7, 2001 • Man's Death of "Bird Flu" in Hong Kong Rais
Flu Raises Concerns on Economy March 23, 2003 • Preparing for the Bird Flu December 19, 2003 • Thais Infect
2004 • Human Spread, a First, Is Suspected in Bird Flu in Vietnam February 2, 2004 • Lethal Strain of Avian F
3, 2004 • Thais Suspect Human Spread of Bird Flu September 28, 2004 • W.H.O. Official Says Deadly Pandemi
Avian Influenza in Japan December 23, 2004 • True Toll of Avian Flu Remains a Mystery March 15, 2005 • Whe
2005 • Danger of Flu Pandemic Is Clear, if Not Present October 15, 2005 • Europe Steps Up Efforts to Stop Av
Hinder Drive to Stop Bird Flu at Its Source November 3, 2005 • New Homosexual Disorder Worries Health Offi
Stirs Fear on Blood Supply January 6, 1983 • Concern Over AIDS Grows Internationally May 24, 1983 • Disord
as a Worldwide Health Problem November 29, 1983 • New U.S. Report Names Virus That May Cause
January 1, 1985 • AIDS Victims Are Targets of New Rules in Britain March 23, 1985 • Immune Deficiency Disord
Called Free of AIDS August 1, 1985 • Health Officials Plan Global Drive to Fight AIDS September 29, 1985
AIDS Cases in U.S. Expected to Rise May 7, 1986 • 71 AIDS Cases Reported in India February 15, 1987 • 1
U.S. March 9, 1987 • AIDS Peril Worries Soviet Leaders April 6, 1987 • AIDS: The End of the Beginning Decemb
Now Exceed 100,000 June 25, 1991 • A Casualty Report: AIDS, Fatally Steady in U.S., Accelerates Worldwide
AIDS Cases Estimated at 4 Million July 2, 1994 • Severe AIDS Effects Seen on Population in Africa
Drop 19% in U.S., in Part from Newer Treatments July 15, 1997 • New U.N. Estimates Double Rate of Sp

HIV "Explosion" Seen in East Europe and Central Asia Novembe